Overcoming Common Problems

EDITOR'S PREFACE

The books in this series have been written to give help on a wide range of emotional problems which we encounter in everyday living.

The aim of the series is two-fold. First, to convey what is known and what is still not known, in a balanced and realistic way. Secondly, to show what help and relief can be hoped for and how problems can be better understood and made easier to live with. Each book has been written in a simple and direct style by a doctor with special knowledge in the field. It is hoped that the series will help the reader to realize that many other people have similar difficulties and as a result feel less isolated.

The first books in the series deal with hypochondria, sex, feelings about childbirth, insomnia, shyness and anxiety, and depression. It is intended to build up a comprehensive series covering a number of themes relating to common problems of modern life with the emphasis on practical help and guidance both to the sufferer and to those close to him or her.

Dr Alan Kerr

SHYNESS AND ANXIETY

Overcoming Common Problems

Overcoming Common Problems

SHYNESS
AND ANXIETY

Dr Phyllis M. Shaw

SHELDON PRESS
LONDON

First published in Great Britain in 1979 by
Sheldon Press, Marylebone Road, London NW1 4DU

Filmset in 'Monophoto' Plantin 11 on 12½ pt. and
printed in Great Britain by
Richard Clay (The Chaucer Press), Ltd.,
Bungay, Suffolk

ISBN 0 85969 136 5

Contents

Acknowledgement

Thanks are due to Barrie and Jenkins Ltd for permission to quote from *The Small Bachelor* by P. G. Wodehouse.

I

Introduction

Ask anyone to describe a shy person and you will probably get an answer like this: 'Someone quiet, who cannot easily join in what is going on and who is, perhaps, hard to get to know.' Whether the speaker is shy himself or not, this is a sympathetic rather than a critical comment. Yet if you ask a shy person for a description of *himself* the reply would be quite different: 'I feel everyone is looking at me, thinking how foolish I look, blushing, stammering and unable to say anything interesting or funny.' And, because it never dawns on a shy person that others suffer but put on a show, he might go on to say, 'Everyone else can make jokes and enjoy themselves.'

Many people go through life like this, assuming that they are the only ones who feel unhappy in the company of others. Eventually the effort of trying to get to know others becomes too much, so they give up trying, and may become lonely and bitter. Agony columns in magazines and newspapers, and radio phone-in programmes carry their tales of unhappiness. Though these people who ask for help may not actually be shy, they are certainly lonely, and loneliness is inextricably tied up with shyness.

Any social or community worker knows how much loneliness people can suffer. So many of their clients say, 'I never seem to meet anyone,' 'I find it so difficult to make friends,' or 'I have always been so shy.' One reason that the Beatles' songs were so popular is that they vividly describe some well-known human problems, sometimes those that people do not usually talk about. One of their best-known hits asked, 'Look at all the lonely people—where do they all come from?' The answer is probably from many walks of life. For every person who writes to Marjorie Proops or phones a radio programme, there may be two who are too self-conscious even to write or dial.

Although shyness and loneliness are very common, those who suffer from them almost always assume that the problem is in themselves and that it is nothing to do with circumstances. People feel ashamed to admit that they have no friends, or that they never go out in the evening, as if somehow they were to blame. Too readily they assume that they are not very nice people and so nobody wants to know them. Yet the first step to understanding the cause of shyness is to admit that there *is* a problem. It is only then that you can try to do something about it. In this book I am going to look at various aspects of shyness, trying to see how much it has to do with the shy person and how much with the society we live in.

Our society has changed fast and dramatically over the past two hundred years, and even more in the last generation. Gone are the days when even London was a collection of villages, each with its own distinctive features, where people could at least recognize many familiar faces while shopping in the local high street. We now have large impersonal towns and cities, people frequently travel miles to work and may live in new dormitory suburbs where it is difficult to generate community life, or even to get to know your neighbour. The centres of many towns are dead hearts, filled with offices and shops, where people work but don't live.

Two hundred years ago it was easier to be part of a

community. People worked in their homes, or at least nearby, and there was less differentiation between work and leisure. Husbands and wives often worked together with their children, unlike today's family where young women with small children are alone for many hours a day.

When you think of all these social changes it is easy to see how much more difficult it is to meet people these days and it is not all our own fault if we have not succeeded. This is an aspect of shyness that we shall be looking at again later on.

The word shyness covers a multitude of different anxieties and difficulties. We are not born knowing how to get on with others, we learn it from our parents, relatives and neighbours throughout childhood and adolescence, and sometimes this is done imperfectly, leaving us feeling embarrassed and awkward later in life. Some people, for instance, know what they want to say to someone but are too anxious to say it, so they panic. Others desperately want to make contact with others but simply do not know what to say. Others know what to say but can't find the words. Some people can say 'hello' and then get stuck over what to say next. Others cope easily with small talk but dry up in embarrassment when something a little more personal is required; they will have many acquaintances but no close friends and at the other end of the scale are people with one or two close friends but no acquaintances.

There are many ways to meet people and get along with them, but since we are all different, we all want different things from our social life. It is important that you decide what you want before you set about looking for it, whether it is group activities or country walks with one good friend.

But what if you seem to put others off and don't know why? Is it related to the way you feel about others? Do you cope with fear or anxiety by looking detached or bored? Do other people sense some underlying hostility of which you, the shy person, are barely aware? Whatever the cause it is important that you know what it is you want to express and how to express it—even if it is disagreement.

Finally, there are the loners. When they look back they realize they never had a close friend or social activity at all. For these people life can be particularly cruel because although they feel something is missing from their lives they don't know what it is.

So shyness and loneliness relate to the general conditions in your society and way of life, to what sort of person you are and to the way you have learnt to express yourself to others; but it can also be related to changes in your life. You may have been fine as a child, then felt overwhelmed and unable to make friends at secondary or grammar school. Or you may have made friends easily with your own sex and found difficulty with the opposite sex. Perhaps you were fine until, because of a job or marriage, you left the town where you were brought up. These sorts of changes—some of them universal, such as growing up and leaving home, others of a more individual kind—call for adaptability and the confidence to adjust to a new situation. Some people fail, and need particular help at times like these.

When you have explored and tried to understand these and other aspects of social difficulties, it will be easier to see what kind of remedies there are. A better understanding of what sort of person you are may be enough. Sometimes there may be practical remedies and, less often, you may need expert help.

4

2

How We Learn Social Behaviour

We have looked briefly at some of the ways you can regard yourself as shy and some of the reasons for becoming shy. Now we are going to look at these reasons in more detail and suggest some ideas to clarify this so far rather vague problem. When you go to the doctor with a pain he will ask you a number of questions to learn more about it and what may have caused it. Questions are just as important when you are dealing with shyness. In general, shyness means a feeling of unease in situations involving other people, and although this describes the way you feel it says nothing about the sort of situation, why you feel as you do, or whether what you feel is in any way apparent to others. Clearly, since anything involving another person is a two-way process, this second consideration is going to be very important. If you are trying to get to know someone, it will make a difference whether or not you go up to them with a friendly smile and say 'hello' or look at the floor shuffling your feet hoping they will start the ball rolling. If they do take the first step, you may be able to respond in a way that will lead to more talk and engage their interest. Or, by failing to look, staring too hard or muttering inaudibly, you may kill the interchange stone dead, and be only too aware of what you have done.

On the one hand, there are your own feelings, attitudes and expectations in a social situation and on the other, there is your social behaviour, or social skills as it is often called, and its effect on others.

But what do we mean by social behaviour? In the most general sense it is what you do when you're with others, and it can even include situations where the others are not aware of you at all, such as in a queue or at a party. In the queue there may be no verbal interchange at all, yet this type of situation can still be social because you are still aware of the others and wondering about their thoughts, reactions and what sort of lives they lead. They may wonder the same about you. Many people are quite untroubled by this process of mutual scrutiny, but others are acutely uncomfortable just walking past people, and they may show it by the way they walk or the expression on their faces. When we become involved in the use of words these non-verbal aspects of our behaviour become increasingly important, as we shall see later on.

It is clear that very little verbal exchange and little interaction go on when we buy something in a shop or buy a ticket on the bus. The same applies to sitting in an office or factory with others. Nevertheless these situations may give rise to acute anxiety. We become more involved in, say, a coffee break, or if we have to ask the boss about time off, and yet more if we have a job interview or go to the pub with a friend. Parties, formal dinner parties, or meetings where we are expected to take part, all demand more of our social skills resources and, finally, there are those situations when we're making friends or finding a serious partner of the opposite sex.

I have purposely arranged these examples in some kind of order to bring out some essential differences in people's individual anxieties. You may recognize those that have greater or less difficulty for you. Social situations may be entirely non-verbal, entirely verbal or, more usually, both. There may be minimal and casual interchange. It may be limited to a particular transaction, such as saying good morning in the street, where there is a fairly clear ending recognized by both parties. The situation may be informal, like the coffee break, or more formal as in asking the boss for time off. It may be structured or unstructured, as in an interview as opposed to the pub. In other situations, even the formal dinner party, your role is not so clear and there are fewer guide lines. Finally, there is the distinction between the closed and the open-ended encounter. You may go off on a weekend course—a really testing situation for the shy person—but the people you meet you need never see again, and there is no commitment. This is also true of many less taxing situations such as visiting a small, unfamiliar restaurant, or dealing with a car breakdown while on holiday.

As you can see, social situations differ from each other greatly, and each one is going to demand different tactics from your social skills resources. This is why people fear one situation rather than another, although some people find them all painful to some degree.

When we look at the wide range of everyday social encounters in which we are normally involved and then take a glance at a six-month-old baby, we can see that however inept we may feel, we have come a very long way, not just in learning to use our minds and bodies for a host of practical and mental activities, but also in this more subtle domain of social interaction. But what is this learning process?

When we talk of learning many people immediately think of school or of acquiring a special skill such as woodwork or playing the guitar. They may think that we learn only at school, or at least when we are still young, but the success of the Open University, evening classes and government retraining schemes shows that although

7

you may be a little slower to learn as you get older, you're learning throughout your life. At the other end of the scale you may need reminding of how much you learn in infancy and early childhood, before any formal teaching begins, including the subtle skills we all require to get on with people.

Nearly a hundred years ago Sigmund Freud pointed out how important the first years of life are, not just in learning facts and how to do things but also in our attitudes to people. Before we are five we can be influenced in such a way as to determine our relations with people throughout our lives: whether we trust or fear people, whether we are wary of or hero-worship certain types of person who might subconsciously remind us of significant people from our childhood. Freud tended to imply that these influences are irreversible without the prolonged exploration involved in psychoanalysis. Nowadays, although we still believe that early influences are important, we are not so pessimistic about the possibility of change. Human beings have an immense capacity for learning and also for unlearning and relearning, and although parents and significant figures in childhood are the most important influences on our development, there are others who can influence us too.

But before we look at what and how we learn, and at what we mean by social learning, let us look very briefly at a controversy which is sometimes confusing, the so-called nature–nurture controversy, which means how much is determined by heredity and how much by environment.

Ordinary observation shows that tall parents tend to have tall children, dark-haired people dark-haired children, but despite strong evidence in favour of inherited characteristics some psychologists have made considerable claims for the influence of environment, suggesting that given the right education and upbringing any child could be a painter, banker or whatever else a parent wished him to be. The consensus among scientists now is that we inherit a potential which can be realized in varying degrees according to the environmental influences. This can be shown with height, where nutrition is a major determining factor. Intelligence as measured by IQ tests demonstrates this very clearly: children reared in a monotonous, uninteresting environment may increase their IQ by several points if they are moved to a more interesting one.

The inheritance of factors which influence our relationships must clearly be more complicated than the inheritance of eye colour or even intelligence and very little is known yet about this area of human development. It is difficult to devise human experiments in social psychology and we are limited to following, for example, children who have been reared in institutions and then adopted, or those rare cases of identical twins who have been reared in different environments. Animals, too, can provide valuable evidence, though we must be careful not to assume that human infants are precisely the same as, for instance, monkeys. Nevertheless they provide valuable evidence.

Charles Darwin, in his book *The Expression of the Emotions in Man and Animals* first described the importance of signals and their interpretation. An animal may bare its teeth, fluff up its fur, spread its tail feathers or stand on its head in the sand. These signals must be correctly interpreted by another animal of the same species as denoting aggression, sexual display or a warning to keep off. The other animal will then respond according to its physical strength, the balance of its hormones, the presence of food and many other factors. The signals form a language for each species and so it is for ourselves, except that we add language to body movement and non-verbal noises. In some animals this language is part of the original genetic programme, in others it must be learnt, as it must in humans.

A constant feature in the childhood of mammals, including man, is the mother–child bond, a very close relationship in which the infant is nurtured, held closely, protected and comforted. Konrad Lorenz, the founder of modern ethology (the study of animal behaviour) drew attention to the profile of mammalian infants, the large head, high forehead, large eyes and snub nose. These features bring out maternal behaviour in both sexes of the same species. We know now that it is very important for a mother to see and hold her baby as soon after birth as possible so that she can completely accept and love it. Mothers of tiny babies need to be near them just as much as the babies need their mothers, it is entirely mutual.

Professor Harry Harlow has for many years carried out experiments on the social life of monkeys in his laboratory in Wisconsin. In one classical experiment he showed that monkeys who were fed but denied the warm contact of the mother's body grew up unable to relate normally to other monkeys. Depending on the age at which the infants were separated from their mothers they behaved in an excessively fearful or aggressive manner. They were unable also to behave appropriately when they were physically mature enough for courtship and mating. When mothers and infants were kept in isolation from other monkeys the psychological damage was less extreme but present none the less. When the fearful monkey was left with its peers, however, in certain circumstances they helped it to behave normally.

In Cambridge, Professor Robert Hinde has demonstrated the effect of six-day separations of monkeys from their mothers. This does not seem a long time, but the young monkey was always clinging and demanding when reunited with the mother and it was a long time before the relationship returned to normal. The severity of the reaction depended on the quality of the mother–child relationship before separation and also on the way the separation took place. If the mother left the 'home' the result was more serious than if the child was moved.

So for normal social behaviour to develop there must be a reasonably secure basic relationship between the child and its mother or mother-substitute. It is from this 'base' that an infant is able without anxiety to explore the rest of the world, including other people.

In the first year of life the infant depends on his mother for warm contact and regular supplies of nourishment. He will also learn to read her expression, to distinguish her from other figures and to respond to her tone of voice and touch. Most mothers need regular contact with their babies, play naturally with them, pick them up and comfort them instinctively, although variations in maternal behaviour are determined by culture. Many babies, for instance, are carried all day long on their mothers' backs in constant contact and being gently rocked, while others are handled very little. At this time in a baby's life deprivation, extreme frustration, cruelty or rough handling will almost certainly bring about a deep distrust of the world and everyone in it, since at this stage people cannot be seen as separate individuals.

As the baby becomes mobile and begins to distinguish people and understand more of what is being signalled by words, facial expression and body movement, he will also become susceptible to shame and humiliation as well as physical discomfort and fear. He will know if he is being mocked or scorned. At this stage he is actively exploring everything he can reach without discrimination, feeling the texture, tasting, smelling and looking. If he is made to feel that these activities are in some way wrong, his initiative can be damaged, and probably his self-esteem too. Parents who are critical of a small child like this often continue, so that dislike of self is constantly reinforced as the child grows older. The parents behave as if he is bad or dirty and that is the self-image he will develop.

Gradually a child will appreciate that there are rules to be followed; that certain actions are right and others wrong, and that his parents will punish him if he transgresses the rules and possibly reward him if he is 'good'. If his parents feel strongly about right and wrong, even if they do not express what they think, a child will sense that he is out of favour but will feel uncertain of himself. He will probably adopt the rules that his parents have made explicit and make up others where he is not sure. These become internal rules directing what he ought or ought not to do, with their corresponding rewards and punishments, which can be quite elaborate. Many children have rituals according to which they must do things in a certain order before they go to bed, or when they get up, have meals and so on. Usually these fade with childhood, but occasionally they continue, or recur, in adulthood and can be distressing to the individual. These rules, rituals, rewards and punishments are associated with a sense of guilt which has to be allayed by appropriate action. If this feeling is strong, you may constantly worry in later life that you have not done the right thing, or that you will in some way be found wanting by others. This nagging guilt and sense of shame hampers growth of happy relations with others. Just as you may apply entirely different standards of behaviour to yourself than you do to others you may also be as critical of others as you feel your parents were towards you, and you justify it because you have adopted their way of looking at life. A child's attitude to other children will reflect the way he has been treated himself, making him fearful, bullying or scornful on one hand or easy going, confident and tolerant on the other.

As a child, our behaviour is guided or shaped by rewards and punishments in the forms of slaps or cuddles, approval or disapproval, the giving or withholding of love, gifts or fines, and this learning process is called *conditioning*. We can be damaged by too much punishment, too little cuddling, inconsistency and unreliability. We can equally be damaged by too much indulgence and too few rules so that we emerge with an unrealistic view of the world in which everyone is expected to play the indulgent parent. Somewhere in the middle, fortunately, there is a wide range in which we can grow up more or less all right.

Exploration is also important to the young child. By testing everything out with his senses a crawling or toddling infant is learning to recognize people and objects with minimal cues at different distances and in new positions. This urge to investigate is inborn and is pleasurable in itself. The happiest adults are probably those who continue to be curious about the world.

Another type of learning is what psychologists call *modelling*, what is ordinarily known as imitation or learning by example. We are constantly watching others when we are small. Children miss very little indeed, and if they are puzzled, they will make up their own explanations. A child will see how his mother treats an older brother or sister and may expect to be treated in the same way if he behaves similarly. He may imitate a younger child to get the love and attention which is being diverted to the little one. He will watch how mother is treated by father and how his parents behave towards their friends or neighbours. If they are nice to people's faces and critical behind their backs he may become like that too. Colour prejudice and religious intolerance can be taken over so naturally that when the child grows up he is unaware of the source of his attitudes, he merely feels them to be right and natural and never questions them.

Since our parents are the first people we get to know, and because we have such prolonged contact with them, we tend to assume that women are like our mother and men like our father. Although as you grow up you learn how people differ from each other you may still find yourself reacting in a stereotyped way to people of a certain build, age or other quality. This is another way social relations can be distorted. The relationship between our parents is also our first example of marriage. If this is harmonious, you can expect to go on confidently to your own marriage, or you may resolve never to take the risk of going through hell like your mother (or father), not realizing that each might have behaved differently with a different partner.

Finally, it is clear that you are going to have a tendency to bring up your children as you were brought up yourself. Even if you were a rebel as an adolescent, some part will have absorbed the attitudes of your parents and you may be staggered to hear yourself coming out with remarks and comments that you disliked as a child. Sometimes, unfortunately, you are totally unaware of this tendency and the way it is affecting your relations with your children and, later on, their friends.

14

Freud emphasized the importance of our early years and Dr John Bowlby has stressed the need to have a strong early mother–child relationship. Professors Hinde and Harlow's work support this. Until recently the influence of the father was ignored, but now it is being studied and later we shall see how important it is. First let us complete our survey of the family background by mentioning recent studies of behaviour in young infants.

The gradual ordering of the world requires that there should be at least some figures who appear regularly and with whom the stranger can be compared. It also seems that infants experiment with facial expression involving lips and tongue before they start making recognizable word sounds. They probably learn by seeing their movements imitated, usually by their mother, who does this quite unconsciously. Then they learn to associate the sight, the feel and ultimately the particular sound as they learn to lip read. Theoretically, a baby to whom no one ever spoke in infancy might not be able to make up the lost ground. More obviously, the way the mother expresses herself, her vocabulary and pronunciation will all be determinants in the child's later speech.

In the second and later years of life, the presence of other children of a similar age is probably almost as important as the influence of parents. Only children living in social isolation, for instance in the depths of the countryside where there are no other children, may suffer through no fault of their parents. Professor Harlow showed that mother and baby monkey pairs isolated from other monkeys had social difficulties later and this suggests that we need to start our social explorations very young.

A follower of Freud, Erik Erikson, took his work several stages further, tracing human development through the remainder of childhood, adolescence and into adulthood. He has described how through play and work with other children we learn to share, to play games according to rules, develop a sense of fairness, and to consider our own needs within the context of an appreciation of others. We learn to take the initiative, accept authority, take responsibility, stand on our own feet or depend on others as appropriate. These developments in our personality show themselves in our attitudes and social behaviour and can broadly be described as a respect for others and ourselves as individuals, and judgement of what is appropriate in any situation. This is an ideal of mature behaviour, and the foundation will be laid at home if that is the way our family conducts its affairs. However, what you must remember is that even if you start with grave disadvantages, such as taciturn or aggressive parents who gave you little to build on in the way of relationships, the deficiency can be made up at school in reasonable circumstances, and even later if school also works out badly. This is the marvel of the human capacity to learn. It is rarely too late.

3

Learning the Rules

Charles Darwin is best known for his demonstration of how man and other animals developed over long periods of time from earlier forms of life according to biological laws. Less famous, but equally important, is his study of signalling systems described in the book mentioned before, *The Expression of the Emotions in Man and Animals*. He drew attention to the different postures, facial expressions and noises made by animals in varying situations, and how these signs could be interpreted and responded to by other animals. These elements of behaviour constitute a non-verbal language which regulates animal societies. Even in the domestic cat we can see this operating. When your cat jumps on the neighbour's wall he will, particularly if he is a tom exploring the region around his home, survey the scene, cross the next garden, continue along another wall, over the shed roofs, until he becomes aware that he is being watched by another feline from a distance from under a bush in the next garden. At this point he will stop and there will be a period of mutual assessment. The various possible outcomes depend on sex, whether neutered or not, as well as size and determination. The intruder may approach too close, in which case the tom on his own territory will rise to his feet with fluffed-out fur, especially down the spine and tail, his ears will flatten, he may stand broadside on and keep his gaze while emitting low growls. The newcomer may be bold enough to proceed and a full-blown fight may ensue, but generally he will retreat diplomatically while still facing his foe. The defending cat now takes the offensive and if not too threatened his fur will settle, his expression becomes almost nonchalant and he will wait while the enemy retreats backwards paw by paw along the wall. There are many variations on this theme, but in general the point is clear that signs are being made, interpreted and responded to. The same kind of exchange may take place with words between men in a pub which the locals regard as their territory. Any newcomer will be carefully scrutinized but has every chance of being accepted providing he does not offend the local customs, underlining the difference between men, who are social animals, and cats who are basically solitary.

Animal signals have been studied in increasing detail since the pioneering work of Darwin, so now we know a great deal about courtship rituals, feeding the young and teaching them skills, recognizing prey and predators and how animal groups are organized. This is the domain of the ethologists, whose work on animals parallels and complements the social psychologists' studies of man. It is a fascinating field of exploration which produces many ideas useful in understanding human social behaviour.

Animal signals are non-verbal but not necessarily non-vocal as the varieties of bird song, used mainly to announce territorial rights, and the roars of stags in the rutting season demonstrate. Non-verbal signs are immensely important in human interchange despite the development of language and they are demonstrated in all parts of the body; face, head, hands, trunk, legs and feet, in that order of importance. The face of humans is far more expressive than any animal, in particular the eyes and the area around them. Joy, anger, dejection, defiance, contentment and all our various emotions can be expressed by subtle movements of the eyebrows and eyelids, mouth and nose, lower jaw and head and neck. A person may make a welcoming expression or a rejecting one corresponding to the flat ears, bared teeth and ruffled fur of the cat, as well as many far subtler messages to a newcomer, who has to interpret them and react accordingly. Michael Argyle has made a special study at Oxford University of this non-verbal language which we all use. He points out that we can express friendliness, interest and readiness to listen by the appropriate smile, gently raised brow and forward lean with the head inclined. Alternatively, we can block further communication by leaning away, holding our head back and fixing the other person with an unsmiling stare or by looking bored. As important as the expression is the way we sit, stand or walk, the gestures we make with our heads and the movement of our feet.

Argyle has also analysed tone of voice and quality of non-verbal noises, the 'hmms' and grunts we emit, hardly aware of what we are doing. A listener may emit the occasional 'hmmm' to encourage the speaker and indicate he is still listening with interest and too-frequent 'hmms' may show that he is impatient for the story to end.

These listening and expressive skills are part of the basic repertoire of what Argyle calls social skills. Although the examples I have mentioned may seem commonplace and obvious, most of us do these things so instinctively that we scarcely notice them. It is very important to become aware of what is happening in these simple interchanges if you think you are not conveying the appropriate messages or are misinterpreting others, for it is undoubtedly an element in social anxiety. For example, John may wish to express a friendly welcome, but if he speaks in a monotonous, inaudible voice and looks at the floor without smiling, George will see no evidence of interest or friendship. If George knows about John from a mutual friend who says John is shy but a good sort when you get to know him, then he will make allowances, looking more carefully to try to put John at ease. But if he meets John for the first time at a pub or party he may make a snap judgement that he is not worth worrying about.

A person like John, who finds it hard to express himself may, however, get quite a long way by being a good listener. Many shy people find this is a way of getting into some kind of social life. Being a good listener means not just looking friendly and expectant, but asking the right sort of non-threatening question such as, 'How long have you lived around here?' (rather than, 'Have you had an upset with your girlfriend recently?'). Most people feel pleased if they are asked about themselves and some may, after a few preliminaries, launch into more personal disclosures. This brings us to the next stage of how to cope with conversations; not only must you be able to express what you want appropriately and listen to others, but it is also important that you are able to begin and end.

In the old days people waited to be introduced, but now you must have a range of appropriate self-introductions like, 'Have you been waiting long?' when you join a bus queue or as you wait in a cinema queue. 'Have you been here before?' is quite good for hotels, restaurants, camping sites and similar places. Or you can ask for a piece of information such as, 'Can you tell me the time?' 'Where is the nearest loo?' 'Where can I buy some postcards?' In these situations you are not expected to give your name unless you get on so well that you might meet again or join in something together. Where it is usual to be introduced by name, such as at a party, then you would give it—'Hi, I've just arrived. The music's loud isn't it? By the way, my name's Jane. What's yours?'

Knowing when and how to end conversations is just as important as being able to start them and you want to manage it before the yawns or glazed expressions become too apparent. Some people yawn even if they are not bored, so you should look for other clues: eyes as usual are the best guide. If the other person is still looking at you a fair amount of the time with the expectant air we mentioned, then carry on if you feel like it yourself. At a party it is rare that you will want to talk to the same person all evening, so it is important to know how to disengage yourself. If you are with someone, you can say, 'Oh, I see my wife/friend signalling over there,' (if you want to enlarge the conversation you can say, 'Come and meet my husband/friend'). If you are alone but want a change of company you can say, 'Excuse me, I must slip out for a moment,' or, 'I must make a phone call'—these are acceptable even if untrue, provided you do not make it obvious that they are untrue. You may object that this is outright hypocrisy and in a sense it is, but a little reflection on what would happen if everyone said what they felt all the time makes it clear why humans in every society have arranged face-saving gambits like these. Everyone recognizes what is going on, but life proceeds much more smoothly in this way. When you have got to know people and built a basis of mutual understanding then you may indulge in the luxury of being truthful.

By the same token, if someone at a party tries a similar gambit with you there is no need to feel that you have been a flop. They just want to meet someone else. It may happen several times before you settle for longer with someone more congenial and this is simply a matter of trial and error.

Now what about the rest of the time, in between the entrances and the exits? Essentially you get the feel of another person by trying out conversational gambits, rather as in chess, and as in chess the opening moves are stereotyped and the possibilities quickly develop if the players are well matched. Usually initial questions are relatively impersonal ones. Then perhaps you move on to family themes, interests, hobbies and more personal matters providing that the other person appears at ease. What is going on is a session of mutual disclosure starting with the neutral and non-threatening and proceeding by stages until an acceptable level has been reached. You need to match your own disclosures with that of the other. If you say too little your acquaintance may feel vulnerable, since he has given away more. If you say too much he may feel he has to match it and has not reached that degree of confidence. Anxious people may find this matching difficult at first, but provided you keep off intimate or controversial topics for a while all is usually well. Having established some rapport you can then afford to be bolder.

It is also reasonable to use, 'How would I react to that myself?' as a crude yardstick at this stage. No book can give a complete prescription for conversation, but this general theme will naturally recur under different headings right through, especially Chapters 10 and 11 on the Fear of Intimacy and How to Help Yourself.

More than once I have suggested that certain rules of social behaviour are necessary for group cohesion and social stability. All groups of animals have a means of communication to keep them together—fish, birds, cattle or baboons—and man is no exception. We do not always understand what the internal signalling system is, why if one fish turns all turn, how a bird signals to others in its vicinity when a predator appears on the horizon, and we have not studied ourselves for long enough to understand how human societies stick together. We do know from the work of historians and cultural anthropologists that variation between societies is very great, ranging from complete dictatorship or a police state with no independent legal system, to a completely co-operative organization where every individual is valued not just for his contribution to the institution but also for himself and the fulfilment of his potential. There are two principles discerned by social psychologists which operate in varying degrees. One is the principle of dominance and the other of affiliation, or friendly co-operation. In the police state and the autocratic family where the word of the head is law dominance prevails, and the individual's life is ruled by his position in the hierarchy. In its extreme form there is no place for affection, individual feelings or development except in so far as they serve the interests of the system. Such systems always have a degree of instability, because they ignore the affiliative principle which also operates in human societies. Conversely, affiliative groups may be unstable because they ignore the dominance principle, although small groups appear to be able to run on affiliative lines for long periods—typically a large family or village where individuals are known, trusted and respected for themselves, and where leadership is by common consent rather than fear. The stability of any group depends on there being enough people who will respect the rules or be sufficiently concerned for others. Enforcement by the police or by social pressure can only supplement the consent of individuals.

The reason for this apparently irrelevant excursion is partly to demonstrate that human groups differ and that they operate according to rules, whether by dominance–

submission signals, like the cats disputing territory, or the affiliative ones of conversational gambits. Here I hope to point out the importance of concern for the feelings of others, even to the point of face-saving ploys. Many conversationalists indulge in subtle or not so subtle scoring tactics, trying to feel superior by putting another at a disadvantage, a variant of the dominance theme.

The rules of social interchange vary up and down the country, between occupations and, of course, between different racial and cultural groups. They have changed with time, and as society has become freer it is at the same time more difficult for the individual to gauge what is acceptable. Fifty years ago it was easier to mark people by their dress or accent because society was more hierarchical. There were many things never spoken of except among intimates and not always then. Now we question everything, but because people are at different stages along the road of 'anything goes' it is easy to stub your toes by not obeying the unwritten and unspoken rules.

It seems likely that when social laws change fast the level of anxiety in the society increases, and this may show itself in a greater degree of individual stress demonstrated either in psychological or physical ill health or increased violence—we appear to be suffering from both at the moment. Social anxiety, too, may be more common than before, so if you feel like a misfit you're not alone.

We have described the ways of learning as imitation or modelling, conditioning and exploration, using trial and error or straight discovery. Another aspect of learning concerns not so much the method but the content—in other words what is learnt.

Edward Hall has described this very fully in a fascinating book called *The Silent Language*. He describes three basic types of learning: the technical, the formal and the informal, a useful division which can explain why some social situations are more difficult and anxiety-provoking than others. Facts and many skills are taught in a straight unemotional way, they do not have moral overtones and can generally be explained clearly and unambiguously. This type of learning would include book-keeping, wood-work, tying your shoelaces and noughts and crosses. It is only social in the most limited sense, though the interchange between teacher and pupil will be coloured by their attitudes to each other and the topic.

Formal learning is the explicit rules which are taught during childhood as if they were immutable and unquestionable. They have moral value in that to transgress them is morally wrong rather than merely incorrect. Once these included going to church on Sunday, covering various parts of your body and not putting your elbows on the table. Men were expected to open doors for women, offer them seats, stand up when they entered a room and avoid certain words and topics of conversation. People did not go outside without hat and gloves and women did not go into pubs. These edicts covered a wide range of trivial as well as important social activities and although people were more restricted and their behaviour more role-determined they may have been less anxious because they lived within this framework, and much of life was predictable.

If not learnt formally like this, rules are learnt informally, being gleaned by observation, conversation or reading. They can have just as much moral force, and transgressing them can lead to as dire consequences as breaking the formal rules does. These days we are taught little social behaviour formally, so for all kinds of situations from the casual encounter to the interview, we have to rely on other modes of learning, going by the behaviour of others and by our own trial and error. If the models you copy are bad ones, or if your first attempts fail, you may give up and become very lonely. It is this sad situation that we are trying to explore fruitfully so as to encourage you to return to the fray.

4

The Importance of Roles

We saw how social learning comes about through imitation, conditioning and exploration. Role-playing comes into all of these. In early childhood we start imitating parents, older brothers and sisters, visitors to the house and key people in the outside world like policemen or bus conductors. Every child has played at being a shopkeeper, an airline pilot, a nurse or an explorer. Children take turns to be the goody or the baddy, and versions of cops and robbers can be found anywhere. Children will also play at the everyday things they see their parents doing, like making bread, going fishing, looking after the baby and so on. They will do these things with props which resemble or simply represent the objects required in the play. Even solitary children make up their own games and many of these girls and boys are very happy alternating their parts using different clothes and voices as required.

In adolescence, of course, this type of game is no longer appropriate, but role-playing continues in a different form. Young people will try out their powers of leadership at school in class organizations and clubs, or in disruptive behaviour, illicit drug use, shop-lifting and other forms of protest. Most important at this age are the early attempts to try yourself out with the opposite sex. Boys often go around in gangs, seeking reassurance and approval from their peers, and reinforcing each other's real or fantasized exploits. Girls more frequently have a special friend with whom they share their most intimate thoughts and for whom the relationship itself is of great importance. So much then, as later, is undertaken through social pressure that in his heart of hearts the adolescent may wonder if all is well, even if his particular ploy apparently brings success. It is particularly hard if his 'act' continues to bring success in later life, leaving him feeling increasingly alienated and forlorn. Even if he admits that there is something wrong, those closest to him are bound to say in an astonished chorus, 'But you have always got on so well with everyone and look how successful you have been.' They do not realize that this has only been at the expense of never allowing a chink in the pose, never letting a word or expression hint at the sense of isolation within. We shall look more deeply at this in the chapter on intimacy.

When you arrive at adulthood you have experimented quite a bit in childhood play and with different kinds of relationships as an adolescent. Have you learnt anything useful, or was it all just play?

Psychologists have described one of the important factors in learning social behaviour as 'taking the role of the other'. This simply means putting yourself in someone else's shoes, seeing what things look like from his point of view. This is also called empathy, a word used rather loosely, but generally indicating an understanding or sense of another person's viewpoint. Nobody has this ability at birth and, indeed, many child psychologists would say that we are basically self-centred until we are about seven years old. Of course we register that other people respond to us with approval, anger or affection and that this depends to some extent on what we do; if we approach a dog gently and offer him food he will wag his tail, eat and will not hurt us. But if we tear up to him and start hitting him with a stick he will either turn and bite us or run away and not let us near him for some time. But before a certain age we cannot connect behaviour with the state of feeling of another living thing. They are still objects like the red-hot iron we learnt not to touch, only less predictable. It is only later that we can understand that the dog feels friendly, angry or fearful just as we should ourselves (and we only infer this, since dogs cannot talk).

Sadly, for many children growing up with parents who do not or cannot show how they feel, learning to empathize is a tall order. Sometimes it is quite impossible and a person grows up feeling that he is at the mercy of others because there is no way he can find out what they feel or what their attitudes are.

If your parents were withdrawn or taciturn, or resented 'personal questions', it is not really surprising if later on you behave as if everyone else were the same. Some parents seem to assume that others somehow ought to know what they are feeling and what they want and are angry if their frequently confusing signals are misinterpreted. They are frightened to come out in the open because they too were once rebuffed. Families, they maintain, ought to be able to understand without resorting to words.

Let us now look more closely at roles. Erving Goffman, a sociologist well known for many works on human relationships, describes our interactions in dramatic terms in the sense that we are all playing out parts alone or in groups in different situations. A fishmonger, for instance, is a particular type of shopkeeper at work, while at home he may be husband, son or father, and at the local pub the life and soul of the party or a habitual complainer. At various times he may be host, adviser, business partner, guest or secretary of a club. Each person has a number of different roles and usually he behaves differently depending on which one he has assumed. Some roles may take clear precedence over others, such as in a marriage where someone is the aggrieved spouse in private but presents a united front to the visitor.

Various jobs have roles attached to them—lawyers are supposed to be shrewd and rather calculating, but in a different way from car salesmen. People may adopt certain ways of behaving when they train for a job—a policeman must be orderly, polite, dependable, cheerful, patient, resourceful and not subject to ordinary human weakness; a doctor must show confidence, patience and concern; a businessman is supposed to be tough, aggressive and active.

Goffman points out that there is a series of props which go with your role which are more than just manner of speech, expressions and what you say. Clothes, for instance: office workers still tend to wear suits rather than jeans, and solicitors dress more soberly than salesmen. Differences in female clothes are less striking except when it comes to age—older women tend to cover themselves more. Also important are factors associated with roles, such as interests, attitudes, political allegiance and so forth.

I mentioned earlier that we could cut ourselves off from intimacy by role-playing and frequently this is the object of the exercise. It is difficult to be intimate until you are strong enough in your sense of who you are not to feel overwhelmed by another. Adolescents are particularly vulnerable. They long for intimacy but are scared, because as yet their sense of identity is shaky. To defend themselves they act tough, pour scorn on affection and may express themselves through sex rather than love.

These empty experiences may increase the fear, forcing them to distance themselves more than ever from closeness. It becomes easier to adopt roles and miss opportunities altogether, finally marrying someone with whom intimacy is not possible. This is especially true of men, whose detached role is reinforced by pressures from society. This is where sex-role stereotyping comes in.

For centuries people assumed that men and women were totally different, and until the twentieth century the evidence was hardly examined. Only one hundred years ago the philosopher John Stuart Mill was called crazy and irresponsible for suggesting that women should have the vote. Now in this country we have got through a great deal of the outward changes needed to bring about equality of opportunities, but what about the *inward* change? Many people would say that we have a long way to go. Others would ask whether we want that sort of change in any case. Here we meet our old friends nature and nurture again: the feminists insist that there are no differences other than the obvious anatomical ones and those that have been manufactured and maintained by society through generations of child-rearing, and it does seem clear from recent psychological and sociological studies that initial differences between boys and girls are very slight, perhaps limited to boys being more aggressive than girls. The studies also show that mothers behave differently towards boys or girls right from birth. In one experiment, where mothers were given babies to hold and play with but were told the wrong sex, the mothers behaved in the way they thought was appropriate to that sex. Schools, too, have different expectations of girls and boys.

The media reinforce the differences, presenting stereotypes of male aggressiveness, self-confidence and dom-

31

inance, and female dependence and submissiveness. These stereotypes put great pressure on people who lack confidence and do not necessarily want to conform to the models, so you must remember that the media projects the polar opposites of male and female. In between there is room for every sort of variation, and the overlap between the sexes is far greater than the differences at the extremes. Still, society disapproves if a woman is aggressive past a certain point, or if she tries to dominate her husband in public. In private she may be the leader and both partners may be perfectly happy that way, but in public remnants of the stereotypes are preserved. Men are still expected to show decisiveness and be protective towards women, although we know there are plenty of indecisive men who would far rather be protected by a woman than take that responsibility themselves.

For the time being, however, relations between men and women in Western society have probably never been so open or informal, and this is something everyone can enjoy.

5

The Influence of Personality or Who We Are

We have looked at the basis of trust founded on a good relationship in early life that we need for learning to get on with others. We have also described some of the rules of behaviour, and the way that each of us behaves differently according to our jobs, our sex and social status. But so far we have paid little attention to the individual.

Each of us can, in fact, be picked out from a crowd of other human beings by our physical characteristics alone. Occasionally we run into someone, greet them and then recoil, saying, 'Oh dear, I thought you were old Jack,' but the swiftness with which we realize our mistake shows just how well we recognize individual differences. When you consider how finely we can discriminate between people's physical characteristics it is not surprising to find that psychologically we are just as unique. Of course we all look for common attitudes and interests because these make bridges between people, but it is the differences which we find stimulating. In spite of this it is intriguing to see how humans have tended to lump people into groups in various ways throughout history, as we shall now see.

The Greeks regarded themselves, not without justification, as set apart from others, so that all neighbours, however civilized, were labelled 'the barbarians'. Until recently the English regarded everyone on the other side of the Channel as being in some way inferior, and it is not so long ago that all black or coloured people were looked upon as uncivilized 'natives', no matter how much their culture was based on kinder and higher values than our own. Centuries of civilization in India and China made little difference to the disdainful attitude of the average European.

Within individual societies, too, there have usually been hierarchies, so that the landowners, merchants, the army, the clergy, artisans and labourers all had their place and tended to feel that the others were a different class of being, separate from them and either superior or inferior. Religious groups have behaved similarly, treating other sects as if they were the embodiment of evil.

Nowhere is the emphasis on irreconcilable difference more apparent than with men and women—women have been regarded as unclean, the agents of supernatural forces, evil, irrational, fickle and unreliable.

It does not take long to realize that the reason for this division into in-groups who are good and out-groups who are bad is due largely to ignorance and to the universal mechanism of projection, whereby we attribute to others those things we fear or find threatening and uncontrollable. The discovery that members of another class are also likeable and friendly is nowhere better described than by Tolstoy writing of nineteenth-century Russia, a society with a wealthy landowning class supported by a vast proletariat and agrarian populace whom they hardly knew as members of the same species. In his novel *Resurrection*, a member of the aristocracy, Prince Nekhlyudov, discovers this class of common people by visiting the prisons, talking to labourers on his estates and travelling third class on a train to Siberia. The discovery was mutual. Said an elderly workman: 'Well, I bin about a bit, but I never come across a gentleman the likes of 'im afore. 'Stead of a punch on the nut he goes and gives up 'is seat to yer. Seemingly there's gentlefolk and gentlefolk.'

Like class and role, other labels are used to ostracize certain groups: lepers in the Middle Ages, Untouchables in India, Jews in many parts of the world. Nowadays we also talk about 'neurotics', 'epileptics' and 'psychopaths' without being clear that all these people are human beings first and foremost.

These considerations are important for two reasons. First, if you are reading this book you may think that because you find difficulty getting on with others you are different in some particularly unenviable way. You may feel set apart because you suffer from strange symptoms and fears or because you fancy nobody can ever like you. Consequently you may label yourself as 'neurotic', whatever that may mean. Although each of us is unique, paradoxically, it is these symptoms and fears which make us all similar. All of us can be over-anxious and experience strange sensations, feel rejected or self-conscious. Because we seldom mention it, we fancy that we are unique in this negative sense when we are simply demonstrating those features we all have in common.

My second reason for describing the human tendency to pigeon-hole everyone is that I want to talk about the theory of personality type in its constructive and destructive aspects. Certainly from the time of ancient Greece people have tried to classify personalities, and more recently psychologists have worked out detailed systems which they use in personality testing when assessing individuals for education programmes, suitability for certain jobs, industrial retraining and many other situations. They have grave limitations but can sometimes give useful information and are in any case an interesting field for exploration.

These tests give people a certain score on the basis of

their answers to a number of questions. The score could be on a 0–10 scale on a line connecting two opposite qualities of the human personality. We know that some people are extremely cautious, never making decisions until they are in possession of all relevant information. Others may jump to a conclusion after the first piece of evidence and act on impulse. We can therefore have a scale labelled cautious–impulsive and a person may be given a score between 0 and 10—0 being extremely cautious and 10 highly impulsive. Most people will fall somewhere in the middle. This can be done for any number of pairs of opposite qualities you like to choose, such as generous–miserly, organized–chaotic, trusting–suspicious, active–passive, or dominant–submissive. As with the first example more people fall in the middle than at the extremes.

Probably the best-known example of this method of scoring individuals is that of the psychologist H. J. Eysenck. He uses two lines or dimensions set at right angles, one extrovert–introvert, the other stable–unstable. Each person is scored on both these measures from the answers to a standard questionnaire and will find themselves in one of the four quadrants resulting from the crossed lines—stable extrovert, unstable extrovert, unstable introvert or stable introvert. Considering the vast complexity of human beings, this measure is crude indeed, but what it aims to show is quite interesting. The typical extrovert is someone who likes being surrounded by lots of people, enjoys plenty of action, group activities, being the centre of attention and getting on with things. The introvert by contrast is more self-sufficient, prefers a few good friends, enjoys reading and quieter, more solitary activities. The stable–unstable dimension refers to emotional reactivity—do you fly off the handle quickly, are you easily upset by mishaps, disturbances of routine, things people say or do, or do you just take them in your stride?

What use is all this in understanding ourselves? A moment's reflection will tell you that the stable extrovert is the favoured type in our society. The action-man, making swift decisions, jet-setting, enjoying a round of parties and having whirlwind affairs with beautiful women is more commonly found in the media than the librarian who enjoys classical music, goes fishing with his best friend at the week-end, and is faithful to his friendly, garden-loving wife. The advertising media especially reinforce this tendency to the extent where people who already feel out of the swim feel even more out of it. Those endless groups of immaculately dressed people, confidently drinking and puffing in casually relaxed poses cannot do much for the self-esteem of the 'out' group. The problem is that this incessant propaganda almost inevitably makes you feel that this appearance and behaviour is desirable. You are not shown the other side of the coin, dependence on drink, envy, the strain of keeping up with some intangible 'ideal'. How do you know that you really want the sort of life portrayed any more than you really want the new kitchen units advertised? Yet you can be persuaded into thinking that your life is somehow incomplete without them.

Returning to your shyness, are you basically a party-goer, or do you prefer the idea of a quiet meal with a special friend? Do you really mind being on your own at times or do you just feel you ought to mind because people tell you with a touch of pity that you lead too quiet a life? You may like the theatre, concerts, the cinema, museums or art galleries but feel ashamed to go by yourself because you feel everyone will realize that you have nobody to go with and pity you. Going around on your own is another theme we shall return to. What you need to do, however, if you are basically on the quiet side is ask yourself whether you really want a giddy social whirl.

What we are trying to discern, and what the psychologists are trying to discover is what is a person's basic personality? What are you born with as opposed to what you have become through all the influences of environment? We saw that a person has a given range of potential in IQ or height and it may well be so with personality characteristics, so it is no good expecting to feel happy if you try to operate outside your own range. That is why people who choose to work as librarians would be unhappy as high-pressure salesmen and vice versa. Where you have a choice, you should try to choose what is right for your own personality. Once again it is Tolstoy who best emphasized the pitfalls inherent in too narrow categorizations of people:

One of the commonest and most generally accepted delusions is that every man can be qualified in some particular way—said to be kind, wicked, stupid, energetic, apathetic and so on. People are not like that. We may say of a man that he is more often kind than cruel, more often wise than stupid, more often energetic than apathetic or vice versa; but it could never be true to say of one man that he is kind or wise, and of another that he is wicked or stupid. Yet we are always classifying mankind in this way. And it is wrong. Human beings are like rivers: the water is one and the same in all of them but every river is narrow in some places, flows swifter in others; here it is broad, there still or clear, or cold, or muddy or warm. It is the same with men. Every man bears within him the germs of every human quality, and now manifests one, now another, and frequently is quite unlike himself while still remaining the same man.

What we must do then is to seek in ourselves what is right, at least for the present. This ability depends, however, on having some idea of who we are, having a so-called sense of identity. Are we just a collection of roles of the kind we have been talking about in the last chapter, an assembly-line worker, a husband, a good sort in the pub? Or do we feel a real sense of ourselves as a person behaving differently and appropriately in all these situations? There is a particular feeling of rightness or inner solidarity that we have when 'being ourselves' and we may only be aware of this in flashes, because at other times it is overlaid by anxiety about what others think, doing the right thing or being found wanting. If we can capture or recapture from the past that feeling of being 'all right' then we can develop and extend it into other situations. Erik Erikson analysed the growth of a sense of identity throughout childhood and adolescence. First of all he emphasizes the need for trust, as we have done, then the development of a sense of physical competence, of being able to stand and walk on our own two feet, to build things up and knock them down, to dress ourselves and generally to grow in self-reliance. We need to be taken seriously as individuals and come to see ourselves in that way and therefore to take ourselves seriously. We need to feel that we can have influence on others by what we say and by expressing our feelings. We must be able to ask for help without feeling an intolerable loss of face and we need to be able to give help without revelling in the power of putting the other at a disadvantage.

While you are learning technical and intellectual skills, even if it is simply learning to read or write or sew on a button, you need encouragement and the reassurance that you are doing it right. Parents, teachers and friends act as sounding boards against which you test yourself and from whose reactions you form an opinion of yourself. If you are forever being criticized, if you never seem to live up to the implied standards, or are prevented from trying things out because mother or father can do it better, you may end up feeling hopelessly incompetent. Likewise if you are one of those who 'whenever you open your mouth you put your foot in it' you may stop opening your mouth altogether. If parents are too sensitive to the reactions of others they may inhibit you so that you have no opportunity to make your own mistakes. Of course you will hurt people's feelings, make them laugh at you or say something inappropriate, but it is by socially stubbing your toes that you learn to become a social being. Parents who are totally uninterested can damage in another way and then it depends on whether you are able to make contact with others away from home who will challenge and encourage you.

Everyone at some time in their life has a special interest, even if it has been forgotten and overlaid by a grey cloud of other people's expectations. It is hard if that interest is mocked or treated as if it is of no account. Many children like reading or making things and can find no quiet place at home. After many rebuffs and disappointments they give up and their interests may be forgotten. Nevertheless, it is never too late to revive the memories of past pleasures and bring these early skills to life once more. Nowadays there are countless housewives, factory workers and clerks who brighten their lives by learning to make jewellery, write short stories or construct useful things for their homes and, of course, in the process they meet others with the same aim of widening their horizons. This is another theme we shall return to in the chapter on self-help.

Erikson carefully studied the growth of our sense of identity, or who we are. Many people have never thought of themselves as individuals before and it may come as quite a revelation to realize, for instance, that they actually feel guilty about putting their feet up and day dreaming. They have to be doing something all the time and much of this flight into activity is an escape from themselves, from just 'being'. Escape is always possible, specially through television or the pub. However, if you were simply prepared to do nothing occasionally you might discover that you are not such an awful person as you feared.

A socially anxious person may have a special need to find himself since it seems likely that a large part of the problem is the belief not only that he is an incompetent human being, but also that everyone else is superbly competent. The truth is that we are all more or less competent or incompetent depending on how you look at it. We all have our frailties, but they are soon forgotten except in the hypersensitive mind of the shy person, who broods about trivialities that should be left in the past.

Tolstoy has also described, better than I could hope to do, the essential self of a young man, his personality or identity which was overlaid when still vulnerable by the pressures of society. Gradually he rediscovers himself through a chance encounter with a girl he had betrayed and whose life was ruined:

Then he had been an honest unselfish lad, ready to devote himself to any good cause; now he was a dis-

41

solute accomplished egoist, caring only for his own enjoyment . . . And all this terrible change had come about simply because he had ceased to put his faith in his own conscience and had taken to trusting in others. And he had ceased to trust himself and begun to believe in others because life was too difficult if one believed one's own conscience . . . To believe in others meant that there was nothing to decide: everything had been decided already . . . Moreover, when he trusted his own conscience he was always laying himself open to criticism, whereas now, trusting others, he received the approval of those around him.

6

The Varieties of Shyness

First, I want to emphasize how common this problem is and how it can affect absolutely anyone, even the most successful people. For example, internationally known playwright Tennessee Williams, who wrote *A Streetcar Named Desire* said about himself:

> My adolescent problems took their most violent form in the shyness of pathological degree. Few people realize now that I have always been and even remain . . . an extremely shy creature. (Now I compensate for this shyness by the typical Williams heartiness and bluster and sometimes explosive fury of behaviour.) In my high school days I had no disguise, no façade and it was at University City High School that I developed the habit of blushing when anyone looked me in the eyes, as if I harboured behind them some quite dreadful or abominable secret.

This highly personal comment sums up a great deal of what shy people feel. Blushing, the feeling of some unexplained guilt or shame and later, of course, ways of compensating for this feeling of inferiority in relation to others. Blushing is one of the commonest and most disconcerting symptoms that a shy person can have. Nevertheless, good as this comment is, it is for our purposes too general and I want to break the problem down further.

We can divide shy people first of all into those who have been unable to learn social skills, those who have

43

learnt them but are unable to put them into practice through anxiety, and those who have learnt them and are now able to put them into practice almost perfectly, though they still feel shy.

People in the first category have been best described by Michael Argyle, and it was for them that his technique of social skills training, described later, was first devised. They start with a considerable handicap, because not only do they fail to look at other people closely, but they also fail to reveal themselves, since they are either looking away from the other person or their face is so expressionless that it betrays nothing. This means they fail to receive all the information to be gleaned from the non-verbal cues described by Argyle and, because they give nothing away themselves, their companion is also in the dark. This in itself is disconcerting, and even if you are acutely aware of the problem you may be quite unable to do anything about it.

The person who lacks social skills in this way will not watch while the other person is speaking, so he often looks bored. When he speaks himself he probably mumbles, so the other person has difficulty in hearing him, and he probably sounds bored with himself and may be unable to initiate any conversation. This, of course, puts a great strain on the companion, who may simply give up in despair.

Underlying this behaviour there is probably a variety of different emotions and attitudes and almost certainly there is the anticipation of unfriendliness, criticism or even downright hostility from the other person. The sufferer may desperately want to get to know other people but because of his fear he gives the impression that he disdains them. Then even an initially friendly and well-disposed acquaintance may become wary, resentful and

44

finally fed up and unfriendly. This confirms the shy person's suspicion that everyone is unfriendly anyway—the so-called self-fulfilling prophecy which is a feature of so many psychological problems.

So what went wrong with these people in the first place? With some people there may be no adequate explanation. With others it is quite clear that they had very uncommunicative parents and probably a mother who spoke and played very little with her children. She may have regarded her children as a nuisance, to be kept out of the way as much as possible. Or the child may have been brought up in institutions where there was little individual care or tenderness and perhaps he or she was passed from one institution to another without ever being able to form a close relationship. Still, there is no reason why things should not be improved for even these people if they are prepared to persevere. More fortunate are those who have gradually been able to learn social skills but have become inhibited using them, and those who have adequate social skills but still feel shy.

There is probably a large variety of difficulties lying behind this sort of social unease. One is certainly low self-esteem, a failure to accept yourself in relation to others. It may be that you are in some way not as successful as others of your own age, in which case it is better to face it and try to take practical steps than to go on feeling vaguely ashamed but do nothing about it. It's more likely that you are no better or no worse than most people but that you are over-critical of yourself and anticipate criticism from others. This might have been brought about by highly critical parents, and a lasting impression of worthlessness has remained. It may be a generalized feeling extending to everybody, or it may extend simply to a few people, but whatever group is involved it is highly unpleasant. To be more precise, you have failed to develop a proper sense of identity, and there may be a very great gap between the way you see yourself and the way you feel you should be or would like to be.

The question of sense of identity was worked out in great detail by Erik Erikson, who emphasized that our sense of identity is rooted in a number of different social categories. First of all we are a member of a particular sex, something which is only gradually confirmed throughout childhood and adolescence. If we are not treated appropriately as boys and girls (or, again, perhaps it is in some way due to the way we are made) we may end up being unsure of which sex we belong to. This does not necessarily make us homosexual, as many people fear, it is often simple uncertainty about what is our appropriate role.

Next, we are members of a family, which may be harmonious and the centre of our affections or quite different—we may even feel ashamed of our family and be frightened that we may have to talk about them, or we may feel the odd one out in the family and extend this into our adult life. Identity is also rooted in your circle of friends, and if you have no friends then you may feel lost in this particular respect, or ashamed and scared to admit it to others.

Then there is the sticky matter of social class. Whether or not you deny the importance of class, sections of the community do show different patterns of behaviour and you may find yourself in one group when you have been brought up in another with a different pattern of behaviour. This makes you feel uncomfortable, as does having a better or poorer education. Your job, too, is important to your sense of identity. You may not have the sort of job that you would have liked, or felt you deserved. There are many people working in what are called low status jobs, but if their self-esteem is well founded in other ways it will not trouble them.

If there is a great discrepancy between the way you see yourself and the way you would like to be, you are probably unaware of it. The discrepancy may be caused by unrealistic expectations from parents or school teachers—perhaps early signs of academic promise were not fulfilled. Or you may doubt your attractiveness because you had very attractive brothers or sisters with whom you felt in competition. But whatever the cause the sense of failure is almost always present and can make life extremely uncomfortable.

I would like now to look at a rather special group, the people who are said to suffer from social phobia. They are usually socially very competent, but in certain well-defined circumstances they are overcome with panic and the most unpleasant symptoms. The situations are usually eating and drinking with others or meetings where people are seated and being watched while doing something. Social phobics feel much easier if they are able to move around, as for instance in a buffet meal or an informal meeting where people are not seated. When the condition is severe, a person may be frightened even to open the front door lest they get involved in a long discussion or have to invite the person in for a cup of coffee. It may be impossible to have people in the house or to visit others, and work may become almost intolerable.

The unpleasant symptoms include palpitations, shaking, trembling, sweating, needing to pass water, diarrhoea, nausea, vomiting and blushing. The phobic person tends to feel that these symptoms are obvious to other people or that they will become obvious at any moment.

47

Anxiety produced the symptoms in the first place, and now the symptoms themselves give rise to further anxiety with corresponding discomfort. It is this vicious circle which has to be broken in treatment so that the person can control the symptoms at an early stage and they never threaten to get out of hand.

It seems likely that the symptoms suffered by social phobics are present in all of us to some degree, though probably less strikingly, and also it is likely that the rest of us are less distressed by them.

Returning to social anxiety in general, it will now be clear that it can be present from childhood, appear in adolescence, or come on suddenly later in life. Almost everyone suffers from social anxiety in adolescence so there is nothing remarkable about this. What the socially anxious person notices is that his friends and close associates have grown out of their anxieties whereas he has not. This means that a number of people ask for help at about twenty-two when they would have been expected to have grown out of their anxieties. Far from getting better, they often seem to get worse.

It is more rare for the problem to come on later in life, or suddenly, but it may be precipitated by a particular incident—usually something important like eating with a senior person, an interview, a meeting with a girlfriend or any other taxing situation. The symptoms may be limited to that type of situation from then on, or they spread to other situations. In the next chapter we shall be looking at this in more detail, with examples to illustrate the various points.

7

When Things Go Wrong

Frequently severe shyness can lead to other problems and these in turn may lead the sufferer to seek help, so now we will look at the other problems which can occur alongside severe social anxiety.

We can all divide our lives up into certain areas. We have our work, leisure time, marriage or special sexual relationship, and friendships. It is quite clear that people who lack social skills are less likely to be married and much less likely to have friends. You may feel that you have no particular sexual problem but simply have difficulty getting to know someone who would make a satisfactory sexual partner. You may be able to work well but your leisure time will be solitary, and unless this is actually what you want it is unsatisfactory. Consequently, someone without social skills is very vulnerable and even if his work is going well that may soon be threatened. People less shy, and those with social phobia, are less vulnerable than this but nevertheless can have quite distressing problems arising out of the initial difficulty.

John is twenty-two, lacks social skills and also has severe social anxiety. He has had social problems all his life and school was a misery for him. Now he is a technician, working in a laboratory virtually alone. In fact the less contact he has with others the better, because he becomes so anxious that even showing a visitor round his laboratory makes him tremble, sweat and feel sick.

He feels acutely embarrassed about all these symptoms since they interfere with any kind of social interchange.

He enjoys his work and he is good at it, and in his leisure time he amuses himself with electronics. Nevertheless, working is still a strain because he never knows when he is going to have to talk to someone. He cannot eat in the canteen with others or join them in coffee breaks, so he is effectively cut off. The rest of his life is unsatisfactory too. He lives alone in one room and is cut off from the other members of the household. He dreads the unexpected knock on his door and is really only relaxed when it is so late that no one could possibly call on him. He knows another young man of about the same age and similar interests but is far too shy and anxious to get to know him properly. He gets on badly with his mother and has no other relatives. All in all it is a very sad picture.

When I first saw John it was quite clear that as well as his extreme anxiety he did not know how to behave, or if he did he was so anxious that he was unable to put his knowledge into practice. He sought help because he felt depressed and unhappy but he found it extremely difficult to put his thoughts into words. Everything had to be dragged out of him by questions and monosyllabic answers. He had long hair which fell over his face and he looked at the floor the whole time; I never actually saw his face in the first interview at all. He mumbled and his voice was monotonous and deadpan. He presented a very sorry spectacle of despair which had clearly been like that for a very long time. John is a common example of someone so socially isolated that life was really almost intolerable and he was quite severely depressed.

Depression so commonly goes with social anxiety that it is worth considering what we really mean by the term. It is certainly not just the feeling of being fed up which all of us have from time to time. It is a recognized illness and it can very frequently be helped, so it is worth checking whether you are suffering from depression or not. It can appear very gradually in the form of increasing fatigue or listlessness, then may follow sleep disturbance, either difficulty in getting off to sleep, restlessness or waking early in the morning and being quite unable to get off again. You may feel ghastly in the morning and then noticeably better in the second half of the day. Your appetite wanes and you may lose weight. A feeling of loss of interest in everything follows, with weepiness for no particular reason, or a feeling that you are always near to tears. Life may seem just not worth living and finally suicidal thoughts will appear. These may take the form simply of wishing that you were dead, or that you would not wake up, or possibly that you might take an overdose of pills of some kind or another. The thoughts come unbidden and can be very alarming, but they are all part of the illness.

If you suffer from any of these symptoms and they have been going on for more than a few weeks, then you should go and see someone for help, usually your own doctor. If you tell him how you feel he may prescribe you antidepressants, which do not work straight away but nevertheless can be very helpful if you persist in taking them. You may also have a few side-effects but these generally go away and are worth it if you benefit from the drug.

The point I want to make is that severe depression can result from extreme isolation, like John's. He was a serious suicidal risk in the long term because life was so unhappy for him that he could see no prospect of improvement. What we had to do was to treat his depression and try and give him hope, as well as special treatment to help him overcome his social anxiety and lack of social skills.

James was a businessman of forty. He was making plenty of money and was clearly successful. He was married and had a family, and although he described his marriage as perfectly satisfactory it sounded as if he and his wife were rather distant, though this had no bearing on his social anxiety. He had friends and they entertained quite a lot but this was a problem too: one of his difficulties was having meals with people. He could not go out to lunch in the pub with staff without feeling acutely anxious, nor could he have dinner at home with people other than his family, or in other people's houses, without feeling acutely anxious. Meetings had the same effect on him, he would feel absolutely terrified, tense, shaky and frightened before a meeting which he knew rationally he could handle perfectly well. Waiting in his doctor's or dentist's waiting room, or any other situation where he had to wait also made him acutely anxious. His way of dealing with this had been to take large quantities of barbiturates supplied by his doctor, who was naturally getting alarmed at the situation, together with alcohol—a dangerous combination anyway, but especially for a man driving around the countryside. Before a meeting he might have to drink up to half a bottle of whisky so as to cope with it all, and similarly he would have to drink before he had a meal with anybody. He was worried lest he become an alcoholic and was very anxious to stop taking the drugs and to be able to drink socially rather than out of necessity.

There are many men and women like James who are terrified that they will become addicted to drugs or alcohol or both. They see no way of leading a normal life without these props and try as they will they cannot do without them. Nevertheless, they are not true addicts or alcoholics and it is most unlikely that they will ever become really addicted. Once the basic anxiety is dealt with then the problem with the drugs and the alcohol should disappear of its own accord. This fear of addiction or alcoholism is another problem to add to our first one of depression. Mary is thirty-five, married with a family. She has had social anxiety since she was a teenager but has managed to hide it fairly successfully. Even her husband does not know what afflicts her, only wonders why she is sometimes reluctant to go out to the local or to visit friends. She sees her doctor and takes small quantities of tranquillizers. She has not had to increase the dose so she is not worried about addiction. What worries her now is that her husband is doing very well in his business and has now been promoted to the board of directors. This means that their life from now on is going to be rather different. Whereas before Mary could see the occasional friend round the corner or have informal meetings and meals with friends at home, she now has to cope with formal situations. She will be expected to entertain at home more and she will have to go out to formal meals with the other directors and their wives. Her husband may also have to entertain visiting businessmen and may sometimes want to bring them home. Mary feels panic-stricken by the new responsibilities thrust upon her. She still finds it extremely difficult to explain to her husband what her real problem is and is very anxious not to let him down. He, on the other hand, cannot understand her manifest anxiety at his promotion and already feels slightly betrayed; now there is a strain on their marriage.

These are just three ways in which social anxiety can affect the person in other areas of their life. If Mary's husband had had the social phobia instead of Mary, promotion might have created the same crisis for him and he may even have turned it down. There are many ambitious men who seek success until it comes to the point where more entertaining and formality is required. People have even considered giving up their jobs because of it, causing a crisis in the family. A young social phobic may hesitate before a sexual relationship which might lead to marriage, knowing what his or her limitations are and how they may affect a future spouse. People also worry about the effect on their children, since they are unable to take them out and about in the ordinary way.

Social phobia is also likely to be associated with agoraphobia (the fear of open spaces). In fact it seems to be present in about half the known agoraphobics. Agoraphobia afflicts mostly women and affects them so that they become increasingly anxious the further they are away from home or a safe place. They may be perfectly all right with a trusted person like a husband or older child, but on their own they suffer from extreme anxiety and panic attacks. They may even be extremely anxious at home on their own. These unfortunate people become housebound, since the fear is so great they cannot bear to leave their own front doors. Add social phobia to their problems and the situation is a miserable one indeed. Apart from the anxiety, which as well as the symptoms for social phobia may take the form of weakness in the legs and breathlessness, there can be what we call depersonalization or derealization, an unpleasant and alarming sensation where the sufferer feels she is somehow unreal and cut off from the rest of the world. She may feel that she is watching herself, or doing things automatically, that her body has somehow changed shape. Familiar things may look strange and vice versa, the outside world may look brighter or dimmer than normal. Many people complain of a floating sensation when they are walking along, as if they are either walking on cotton wool or their feet are not touching the ground properly. What is striking, however, is that people seldom admit to these feelings spontaneously. The therapist always has to ask the appropriate questions to find out if the client has any of these sensations. This is partly because the sensations themselves are vague and difficult to put into words and partly because they are alarming and people get the idea that they are going mad. If you suffer from this type of symptom, be reassured that it has nothing at all to do with going mad. In fact many people with no other problems suffer in the same way from time to time if they haven't eaten enough, if they are short of sleep or if they have a fever. One could almost say that they are normal feelings but in certain people they reach abnormal proportions.

We can see now that social phobia, upsetting enough in itself, can be accompanied by other problems covering a wide range. If any of them trouble you, you should seek professional help because it may mean that your shyness is severe enough to warrant expert attention.

8

Who Is At Risk?

Now I want to concentrate on the here and now, and the problems of people who, having managed reasonably well up to now despite their shyness, find that their resources are overtaxed and that they are acutely aware of their social distress.

The first group is young people of both sexes leaving home. They may not have made friends at school or in the neighbourhood, and they may well have felt lonely from time to time, but young people can often cope with this providing they are still living at home with their family, especially if they have brothers and sisters. But inevitably the time comes when you must leave home, launch out on your own, go into lodgings or a hostel and cope with work or study. Those who have had no particular difficulties look forward to the challenge of trying their skills in the adult world. Difficult patches are overcome, a satisfactory career is found and with any luck there is a steady girlfriend or boyfriend—all of which leave you feeling reasonably independent of your family, who are now your friends rather than protectors.

Unfortunately, things don't work out so well for everybody. It is one thing to set up house with a friend in a little flat and quite another to take a room of your own in a house where you know no one and no one knows you, as many people do when they go to university or to another town to work.

If you start making friends at work or college then you will start visiting other people and having them back to your room, but many youngsters who have been unhappy and lonely at school think that if they start afresh it will all be different; it is then terribly disillusioning if they have been a whole year and have made no friends at all. A lot of these problems come to a head during the second year away from home, when disappointment is beginning to affect their general health and well-being, and perhaps their work. Then they need to seek help.

Another group at risk are mothers with small children. This is a very difficult time in a woman's life. She has probably stayed working until her first pregnancy, and is delighted at the idea of having a baby, which is what both she and her husband had wanted. But she may not realize the full impact it is going to have on her life. From the moment the baby is born she cannot move freely, she cannot go out when she feels like it or leave the house for long enough to pop across the road to visit a friend. Babies do not need full-time care, but they certainly need full-time responsibility. Through sheer convenience, the young mother will stay at home more than she did before and when the next child comes along she will continue to stay at home. Many women are good planners and take their babies everywhere, but others find it more difficult, and spend more and more time at home.

By the time her children reach school age she may have become so turned in on herself that she is frightened to take the child to school in case she meets other people. If you are rather shy anyway, when you are cut off from human companionship for any reason then it is far more difficult to get back into the swim again. Confident people will simply start making new friends, but the less confident will tend to hope that someone will notice them rather than take the initiative themselves. A husband can help here by encouraging his wife to ask people to drop in in the evenings or at the weekends when he is there to lighten some of the social burden. He can also encourage his wife to keep up with her former friends as much as she can. In any case, as much outside contact as possible should be maintained: in this case prevention is far easier than cure.

The same thing applies to older women whose children are growing up and leaving home. A woman who has been a devoted housewife and mother and spent little time on her own activities or with her own friends feels an enormous void when her children finally leave home. Clinging to them produces resentment, so she often feels rejected and loses her self-esteem, which is quite inappropriate. At this time, too, a woman needs her friends. Her husband may very well be reaching the peak of responsibility at work and his interests may be more outside the home than inside. While this leads to greater responsibility for his wife and greater involvement with her children it also leads to greater isolation. She has to beware of becoming cut off from friends and outside contacts, and now is the time to pick up the threads again if they have been dropped earlier.

We hear a great deal now about the loneliness of isolated old people but less perhaps than we should about the contribution to this loneliness made by shyness. Old age is basically a problem of retirement and gradual disengagement from society while at the same time making the very best of what is left of life. If husband and wife both remain alive and can live through the husband's retirement together they can tackle their problems jointly and support each other, but for those who have never married, and those who have lost a spouse, it can be very difficult and tragic. The single shy person may have been sustained throughout life by a satisfying job, or at least the feeling that he was doing the job well. Contacts at work may have been just sufficient social stimulus to keep him going. When that is gone, what is left? He may hardly know his neighbours because he has been out all day working and perhaps he enjoys gardening at week-ends, another solitary occupation. Similarly, the bereaved person may have been supported through life by a spouse to their mutual advantage—but not to the advantage of the one left behind if the other should die.

These people may have to start afresh, and it is very difficult to begin making friends at the age of seventy. It is not surprising that many elderly people do not make it, and later we shall look at what can be done to help them.

Some shy people select their jobs specially so that they will not come into contact with people or at least only at the most superficial level. These are the backroom boys, technicians who work largely on their own, lorry drivers, meter readers and many other groups who have minimal contact with others. They are, of course, unknowingly simply making their problem worse, because the more they avoid people the more difficult it is going to be to get back into contact with them. Some people, as we saw in the chapter on personality, don't particularly want to be in the swim and don't feel that they are missing anything, but there are certainly those who regret that they have become cut off and are anxious to come back into society again.

I have already mentioned promotion, which may put a very great strain on the man who has been promoted and his wife who is going to have to adjust her standards to the new life. The same applies if a woman is promoted, but it is a problem more commonly associated with hus-bands' promotions. Any movement upwards in the hier-archy, whether it be teaching, business or any other walk

of life, almost inevitably means more publicity, more formality, more social occasions on which you have to be on
your best behaviour. For the man it will also mean more
meetings, and more entertaining where he must know the
right approach. His wife will almost certainly start worrying about her clothes, her appearance and the way she
presents herself in public. Both may be anxious about
their accents and the way they speak. It may have been
perfectly acceptable to have a broad dialect while still in
the ranks, so to speak, but moving up means meeting a
different sort of person who speaks and behaves differently, who is used to eating out in good restaurants and is
familiar with other ways which the newcomer is not used
to.

Then there are people who have dropped out of society
for various reasons and who are trying to get back in
again, such as people who have been alcoholics, drug
addicts, in jail or borstal and who face a period of rehab-
ilitation with a stigma attached to them. In an ideal
society, of course, it should not be like that, but unfortunately many people are still seriously prejudiced
against these groups.

Immigrants' problems are so great they need a book on
its own, but I mention them here for the sake of com-
pleteness. Not only do they face a different language and
religion, but also a whole range of social behaviour built
up on entirely different lines. I can only say briefly that it
is up to the host country to make the transition as smooth
as possible.

9

Coping with Catastrophe

Some people who have never regarded themselves as particularly shy discover at some stage following a crisis in their life that it is difficult to make relationships with other people or even to approach them. Sudden bereavement in early or middle life, the arrival of a congenitally handicapped child, redundance and other events which change circumstances may bring on a form of shyness or social anxiety.

Mrs Thomas had lived with her husband in the Middle East for fifteen years where he had a job with an oil company and was used to going to social functions with or without her husband. She was not particularly happy there, but she felt she was probably as well there as anywhere else, since there were advantages. When their boy reached school age, Mrs Thomas brought him back to Britain to find him a school and set up home for him over here. This meant a total change in her way of life. Her son went as a weekly boarder to a local school and she found a house in the same town, one she had never lived in before, and she saw her husband very infrequently. In some ways this was no bad thing because relations between them were strained, but Mrs Thomas found, much to her surprise, that she was quite unable to go to school functions such as parent–teachers' meetings, plays or anything else that went on at the school. Although she had spoken to her neighbours she could not pluck up enough courage to invite them in for a drink or a cup of coffee. She could not think of ways of making friends because she could not make the first move. It was after two or three months of this that she finally sought help. She was a sensitive person and it is quite possible that she was more shy and dependent on her husband than she had admitted to herself. Nevertheless, this was a very striking change for her.

Mr French had worked with the same engineering firm for thirty years and was now fifty-five, married with four children. He was appalled to find that he had been made redundant. Two of his children were still at school and only one was earning, the other one was still at college. His wife had a good job and he had quite a bit of money saved, but this was not the point. Finding another job at his age was difficult, so out of the blue his working career, through no fault of his own, was cut short. The blow to his self-esteem was incalculable and he turned in on himself, going into his shell and finding it extremely hard to meet people any more. He stopped going to his local, he was reluctant to take his wife out for meals and even nervous about taking the family on holiday.

Mrs Fisher had been happily married for twenty-five years when suddenly her husband died of a heart attack. She was only forty-two, very attractive and used to getting on socially with no problems at all. Her husband had had quite a public position and she had accompanied him to many formal functions which she did not fear in the least. Now she found she could not make up her mind about anything, she dreaded meeting people she knew and she avoided her neighbours. She became more and more socially isolated until finally she sought help. She suffered from a sense of disorientation, as if her whole life had collapsed—which in some respects it had. She had married at seventeen and had gone to her husband straight from a rather unhappy home. In one sense he had given her everything, and now that he was gone she did not know what to do, so greatly had she depended on him. She had never formed the habit of taking the initiative herself and, like Mr French, her self-esteem suffered. To her, being married was the only possible way of life, since she had been married almost since childhood. To find herself unmarried made her feel inferior, somehow not as good as other people.

You will see from these stories that although only one of them was bereaved in the strict sense, a sense of loss was involved. Mrs Thomas lost her familiar surroundings, her husband and her usual way of life, Mr French lost his job after thirty years. Shyness, although it was quite a prominent feature, was only part of a general need to reorganize life.

It will be helpful to look at these situations in more detail and examine other situations which can unexpectedly give rise to shyness. The people who fall into these groups are generally middle-aged people who have coped well with life until a crushing blow, which will take at least two years to adjust to. Not everyone reacts in this way, of course, some people become intensely anxious, other people can't sleep, others lose weight and some become very depressed. A loss of any kind is going to lead to some degree of depression and this will usually take the form of loss of interest, energy and sleep.

What does it mean to be bereaved? In this context I am talking about bereavement in early or middle life, since in late life the situation is different. Then you expect people to die and your friends to thin out gradually. But death in early and middle life comes as a very nasty shock. When someone in their thirties or forties dies they often leave behind a young family with all the responsibilities that entails. So as well as losing a loved partner in the prime

63

of their life, you need to take on double the responsibilities, including financial responsibility.

When the first shock is over the bereaved person has to look around and try to gather his (or, more commonly, her) resources. She may find herself in difficulties with relatives who are not prepared to help as much as could be expected. She may also find herself suffering from a tremendous sense of injustice and envy of neighbours who still have their husbands. She may find herself being excessively defensive on her children's behalf without realizing it. Generally friends and neighbours want to help but do not know how to start and unfortunately it is up to the bereaved person to make the first move. A woman who has a good relationship with her own family is probably in a better position to deal with this than one who is isolated. Nevertheless, at some stage moves have to be made because it is often impossible to carry on without some help until finances and other practical matters have been properly sorted out. This may take a lot of time and cause much anxiety.

If you find yourself in this situation and you have good friends and neighbours do not hesitate to ask them if you may call in and talk to them, they will be only too pleased for the most part. They would want you to do this in any case but would be frightened of interfering and therefore have not invited you. If you know anyone else who has been through the same experience this will be immensely helpful. There is also an organization called Cruse for people who have been bereaved and who can help each other. You are going to need every practical prop you can lay hands on in the next few years, so you must seek help from the Social Services. It is best to begin early to sort things out.

In this situation shyness takes the form of an inability

to ask for help. Whereas before you had been able to hold up your head with self-respect, asking help when needed and giving it in return, you now feel like a beggar because you have so little to offer in return for what you feel must be a great deal to ask of anyone. Try to share the burden between various friends and remember that one day they may need to call on you for help.

Most of this advice also applies to separation and divorce. In many cases it may be a relief that a stressful partnership has been broken up, but sometimes the one who is left behind may have had little idea that there was anything wrong. There may also be very complicated legal considerations to be sorted out, dragging on for many years. Here, too, people have trouble asking for help, tending to lose their self-respect and finding it difficult to confront society as a single person instead of a member of a partnership. You have to remind yourself time and time again that other people are well-meaning but ignorant. They do not know how to cope with your situation, they realize how grave it is and would like to help but are frightened all the time of interfering and putting a foot wrong. This is why bereaved, separated or divorced people sometimes complain of being shunned or avoided. If this is true, then it is simply defence put up by others because they do not know how to handle the situation. If you can show someone how they can help then generally they will.

It may take years to get over this kind of shock; many people have estimated it as at least five years, with two years to get over the worst. An American investigator has made a scale of stressful events in people's lives—incidentally, these may be pleasant as well as unpleasant events—and top of the list were bereavement, divorce and separation.

I mentioned earlier that there were circumstances when you now need to take the plunge alone, where previously you always had company. This applies not only to approaching friends and neighbours for help, but also to going out in the usual ways for trips in the country, restaurants, bingo, cinemas and so on. Now that you may have to do these things on your own, you may feel in some way ashamed that you are seen by yourself. This will not last, however, and you may even find certain compensations which you could not have foreseen. When you meet new people and make friends you know that you are accepted for yourself rather than as half of a pair, and now you can do what you want without having to consider another person's likes or dislikes. No matter how good a partnership, there are always differences of taste, and there are probably a number of activities you have given up for the sake of peace. Now you can pick up all these things as well as developing new interests.

You may feel that couples will not welcome a single person, but this is rare and mostly the reservation is on the side of the single one. You no longer need to worry whether a new friend will get on with your partner, a difficulty even in close relationships unless there is an agreement that you each have your own friends.

So although nothing can make up for the loss of a loved one, there are ways of making the best of a situation rather than the worst.

Surprisingly similar results follow other events which can befall you. The first that comes to mind is the arrival of a handicapped child in the family. When this happens, the sense of desolation and horror can be immense. It may be virtually impossible to accept the child and then, of course, there is the corresponding guilt and an immense blow to self-esteem. This is another situation where others are not very good at helping and unfortunately it applies as much to those working in a professional capacity as to friends and relatives. People with the best will in the world simply do not know what to say, they do not know how to comfort you, especially where it is a question of whether or not the child should be brought up in an institution. The parents themselves are generally so mixed up about it that whatever an outsider says is wrong. It is another situation where a person previously not shy may become almost a recluse, and, once again, friends have to be told how they can help. Sometimes taking your troubles outside the home, where emotions are not so highly charged, is better, and talking about it can be an immense relief.

Other situations include physical catastrophe from outside, such as assault, burglary or an accident, and although these might seem obvious cases where friends and neighbours could rally round, yet again we find the familiar problem that they are frightened of interfering and worry that they will say the wrong thing. Once again, the sufferer has to make the first move.

Moving house is another time when people not previously shy may find themselves over-anxious about making new relationships. This cannot, of course, be rated as a catastrophe unless it has meant coming down in the world and having to put up with something far less comfortable. In the ordinary way it accompanies a promotion, change of job or a posting to another town. Most people cope with the transition surprisingly well, but others have difficulty overcoming the break in their lives. If you are going straight into another job it is not too difficult to start making friends at work, but for the wife who is at home all day, perhaps with small children, the situation is more grave. She has to pluck up courage to talk to other women at the shops or get into conversation when she is picking up her children from school.

In these situations, where people suffer losses, blows to their self-esteem or interruptions in their usual way of life, there will be a variable time in which to make an adjustment, but they all have one factor in common, that the person new to the situation must decide what he or she wants, and take positive action; it is no use waiting passively on the sidelines hoping that somebody will come along with a solution. Once you have decided what to do you can almost always find people to help you.

10

The Fear of Intimacy

It has been said that in this century we are less frightened of sex than we are of affection. It is true that while most people have some kind of physical relationship (which may or may not be entirely satisfactory) fewer have intimate relations. Intimacy implies that you have been through the early stages in making a relationship that we have discussed so far, and have got to a point where you want to know the other person more deeply and are prepared to reveal yourself more fully as well. We are mostly very frightened of revealing the 'real I' and because of this we miss a great deal of life, including the satisfaction of being deeply involved with a number of other human beings. It is lack of intimacy that is behind the dissatisfaction many people have with their sexual relationships. Sex becomes a mechanical, physical act which has no basis in a profound respect and understanding of the other person and the knowledge that you are also understood and respected. But why are we so frightened of revealing ourselves to our fellow human beings.

The clearest situation where this fear of affection and intimacy happens is between the sexes, so I shall deal mostly with that, though some of the points apply to same-sex intimacy. I will start by giving a rather long quotation from *The Small Bachelor*, by the late P. G. Wodehouse. This particular episode occurs at the beginning of the relationship, and it brings out many valuable points.

The chief drawback to being a shy man is that in the actual crises of real life you are a very different person from the dashing and resourceful individual whom you have pictured in your solitary day-dreams. George Finch, finding himself in the position in which he had so often yearned to be—alone with the girl he loved—felt as if his true self had been suddenly withdrawn and an incompetent understudy substituted at the last moment.

The George with whom he was familiar in day-dreams was a splendid fellow—graceful, thoroughly at his ease, and full of the neatest sort of ingratiating conversation. He looked nice, and you could tell by the way he spoke that he was nice. Clever, beyond a doubt—you knew that at once by his epigrams—but not clever in that repellent, cold-hearted modern fashion: for, no matter how brilliantly his talk sparkled, it was plain all the while that his heart was in the right place and that, despite his wonderful gifts, there was not an atom of conceit in his composition. His eyes had an attractive twinkle: his mouth curved from time to time in an alluring smile: his hands were cool and artistic: and his shirt-front did not bulge. George, in short, as he had imagined himself in his day-dreams, was practically the answer to the Maiden's Prayer.

How different was this loathly changeling who now stood on one leg in the library of Number 16 Seventy-Ninth Street, East. In the first place, the fellow had obviously not brushed his hair for several days. Also, he had omitted to wash his hands, and something had caused them to swell up and turn scarlet. Furthermore, his trousers bagged at the knees: his tie was moving up towards his left ear: and his shirt-front protruded hideously like the chest of a pouter pigeon. A noisome sight.

Still, looks are not everything: and if this wretched creature had been able to talk one-tenth as well as the George of the day-dreams, something might yet have been saved out of the wreck. But the poor blighter was inarticulate as well. All he seemed able to do was clear his throat. And what nice girl's heart has ever been won by a series of roopy coughs?

And he could not even achieve a reasonably satisfactory expression. When he tried to relax his features (such as they were) into a charming smile, he merely grinned weakly. When he forced himself not to grin, his face froze into a murderous scowl.

But it was his inability to speak that was searing George's soul. Actually, since the departure of Mr Waddington, the silence had lasted for perhaps six seconds: but to George Finch it seemed like a good hour. He goaded himself to utterance.

'My name,' said George, speaking in a low, husky voice, 'is not Pinch.'

'Isn't it?' said the girl. 'How jolly!'

'Nor Winch.'

'Better still.'

'It is Finch, George Finch.'

'Splendid!'

She seemed genuinely pleased. She beamed upon him as if he had brought her good news from a distant land.

'Your father,' proceeded George, not having anything to add by way of developement of the theme but unable to abandon it, 'thought it was Pinch or Winch. But it is not. It is Finch.'

His eye, roaming nervously about the room, caught hers for an instant: and he was amazed to perceive that there was in it nothing of that stunned abhorrence

71

which he felt his appearance and behaviour should rightly have aroused in any nice-minded girl. Astounding though it seemed, she appeared to be looking at him in a sort of pleased, maternal way, as if he were a child she was rather fond of. For the first time a faint far-off glimmer of light shone upon George's darkness. It would be too much to say that he was encouraged, but out of the night that covered him, black as the pit from pole to pole, there did seem to sparkle for an instant a solitary star.

'How did you come to know father?'

George could answer that. He was all right if you asked him questions. It was the having to invent topics of conversation that baffled him.

'I met him outside the house: and when he found that I came from the West he asked me in to dinner.'

'Do you mean he rushed at you and grabbed you as you were walking by?'

'Oh, no. I wasn't walking by. I was—er—sort of standing on the door-step. At least . . .'

'Standing on the door-step? Why?'

George's ears turned a riper red.

'Well, I was—er—coming, as it were, to pay a call.'

'A call?'

'Yes.'

'On mother?'

'On you.'

The girl's eyes widened.

'On me?'

'To make inquiries.'

'What about?'

'Your dog.'

'I don't understand.'

'Well, I thought—result of the excitement—and

nerve strain—I thought he might be upset.'

'Because he ran away, do you mean?'

'Yes.'

'You thought he would have a nervous break-down because he ran away?'

'Dangerous traffic,' explained George. 'Might have been run over. Reaction. Nervous collapse.'

Woman's intuition is a wonderful thing. There was probably not an alienist in the land who, having listened so far, would not have sprung at George and held him down with one hand while with the other he signed the necessary certificate of lunacy. But Molly Waddington saw deeper into the matter. She was touched. As she realized that this young man thought so highly of her that, despite his painful shyness, he was prepared to try to worm his way into her house on an excuse which even he must have recognized as pure banana-oil, her heart warmed to him.

There are a lot of things in this lifelike description which are worth noting. First of all, George compensated for his tremendous feelings of inferiority by building himself up into a hero in his own imagination. Not everyone can do this and, as can be seen here, it is not an entirely satisfactory thing to do because you are constantly disappointed by the real thing. There follows a description of his feelings that everything about him is entirely wrong, that he looks repellent and has absolutely nothing to commend him. He has gone from one extreme to the other. After a horrifying gap of silence where Molly is waiting for him to make some kind of introductory remark, he manages to put the record straight by explaining that he has been introduced wrongly by her father. You will gather from this that they have not met

73

but that George had seen her around on various occasions and had already become extremely fond of her. This was a sensible thing to do but did not lead very far. George then looked at her properly for the first time and realized that she was entirely friendly disposed and not feeling the way he anticipated. This is a very important point: as I have stressed, many shy people do not actually look at the people they are talking to, so cannot judge what effect their remarks are having, or how they are being accepted. The problem is not solved simply by one person looking friendly on one occasion, but it does help.

The story continues with Molly taking up the initiative and asking a question. This, of course, makes it very much easier for George who, as he said, was perfectly able to answer questions—his difficulty was in finding new topics of conversation, hence the trouble he has in getting away from the limited topic of his name. Molly then discovers that he had come to visit her and not to see her parents as she had supposed. She actually felt flattered, despite the fact that George was obviously extremely shy; it showed courage for him to be able to get that far. Finally, in this description we are shown how perfectly sane people may say the most ridiculous things in situations of stress. As P. G. Wodehouse says, any psychiatrist listening to his conversation out of context would have thought he was mad straight away. Molly, however, understood the effect that shyness can have on an otherwise perfectly sensible man. The encounter ended happily and their relationship proceeded satisfactorily, but it could have turned out differently: if Molly had not been a sympathetic girl, or if she had been looking for a tough, masculine type, she would have rejected George in exactly the way that he feared. But at the same time George probably would not have become fond of her in the first instance; he must have sensed this particular sensitivity which she had.

Unfortunately, in real life gentle men are sometimes attracted to tough women who really ought to have tough mates and vice versa. It is therefore most important that you try to sort out what sort of person you really want. You may find to your dismay that you are best suited to a type who does not attract you physically. A man may like the idea of a rather docile, dependent female, but when it comes to living with her it is not much fun unless he is happy to make all the decisions. A woman may like the idea of the aggressive male stereotype, but here again living with such a man is a very different proposition. He may take the law into his own hands without considering her feelings, taking her for granted and leaving her all the chores.

Why is it that people are frightened of committing themselves to intimacy? Some people undoubtedly fear others becoming dependent on them, and they know very well that once you have imparted intimate confidences you feel dependent on the person in whom you confided. But far more commonly, you fear revealing something about yourself which you feel may be incriminating. Frequently you have no idea what this is, and it is very important to try and find out so that it can be looked at objectively. Looked at squarely, most of these fears readily dissolve.

Another major worry is that you are not fulfilling your sexual stereotype, and for this we must blame the media and social pressure in general. We saw how this operates in the above quotation. A man believes he must be much tougher than he really feels. A woman may feel she is too intelligent and that intelligence puts men off, or that she is not sufficiently 'feminine'. But what are 'masculine' and 'feminine'? There is no reason why quietness, gentleness and consideration—traditionally 'feminine' qualities should not belong to both sexes, especially since they make it easier for everybody to get on together. Being 'feminine' is supposed to mean being dependent, compliant, unaggressive and happy to be led, yet there are bonuses for a man whose wife is better, or at least as good as he is in certain areas. Responsibility can be shared and each has someone to take an intelligent interest in the other's work or interests. And women who are led into thinking that the feminine stereotype is ideal behaviour for a successful marriage will often find later that they are not really like that at all and have had to put on an act for many years.

Sexual fears also hold people back from full relationships. They fear they may be abnormal, physically or mentally; perhaps they have what they think are unusual fantasies which they dare not admit to a partner. It is fair to say that everyone has sexual fantasies, many of them lurid, but this need not impair a good relationship—it can even be a source of humour if shared, and to admit to it will do no harm. By the way, to have fantasies about sex is different from actually living them out. For every hundred people who have fantasies about tying up and beating a sexual partner, only one will actually go ahead and do it.

A huge number of people fear rejection. Pamela, for instance, was a lively, attractive, intelligent girl who got on extremely well with everybody and made initial contacts easily. After a week or two however she began to be frightened and to start backing out of a relationship, even if she liked the person very much. She could not understand why, but saw there was a danger that if she went on like this she would never form any satisfactory permanent relationships with anyone. Careful discussion showed that she feared that she would bore people and that they would find out she was not as interesting as she initially appeared. She felt she could not bear the hurt if they were disappointed and finally backed out on her, and she was not prepared to take the risk. Further discussion showed that this was precisely the way her father had behaved towards her when she was an adolescent. In one sense he was the most important male figure in her life at that time and therefore extremely influential so far as later relationships were concerned. She described him as having discussed matters with her for as long as he was interested. Then he would suddenly switch off, so she felt she was simply being used, that he was not really interested in her for her own sake at all. Now she was applying this early experience to her current relationships, with disastrous results. Happily, the mere fact of seeing how this had come about her made her able to change quite dramatically and soon she was able to form happy intimate relationships.

There are many people like Pamela who have had unfortunate early experiences either with their parents or with a girlfriend or boyfriend in their teens. Fortunately seeing the situation clearly is usually enough to cure it.

In his pioneering work on family relationships, Freud described the tremendous influence that parents could have on children, particularly in the first five years of their lives. But what he did not do was to describe the way in which parents could change towards their children according to their age, and how parents themselves could have faults. To Freud parents were a fixed part of the scenery, so to speak, and he described only the way in which the child reacted to them. Since then, of course, we have realized very much more what an influence parents can have through vagaries in their own behaviour and failure to respond appropriately to the changing behaviour of their children at different ages. Pamela's father for instance was her first 'boyfriend' and it was terribly important for her to gain his approval. The fact that he did not respond to her adolescent needs for appreciation and encouragement meant that a pattern was set up for her future in which she expected all later boyfriends to behave the same way. Patterns of this kind often determine our adult behaviour, and sometimes they can be sorted out by the individual without resorting to expert help.

What then is a good type of relationship? Perhaps it is best when power is equally shared by the partners so that they both take decisions in different areas of their lives without conflicting. But it is even better if they can discuss things and arrive at a mutual decision, especially over such matters as their children's education or how the family budget should be spent. Also, both partners ought to be autonomous emotionally. By this I mean they can cope for themselves if left alone without needing the other to take decisions for them. This avoids immature dependence on the partner who takes a greater share of the weight of the relationship than the dependent one. Mature dependence, however, is where a partner is happy to be advised by the other and will change his or her mind as a result of this advice. Most important of all is a willingness to consider another's feelings—mutual respect. The more the partners are ready to give to the relationship instead of taking from it, the greater the emotional riches. This includes tolerating the other's interests and hobbies, quirks and idiosyncrasies. If you find certain things intolerable in your partner perhaps you miscalculated when you married, or perhaps it is the sign that something else is wrong—a temporary upset about something important can show itself in irritation over trivia. Partners must be prepared to discuss these differences because it is only by this discussion that they can be resolved. Some people, particularly men, shrink from discussing emotions, saying that they are not interested, and this usually means that they are frightened. By avoiding discussion the gap widens so that finally it is impossible to talk deeply at all, when a leisurely chat earlier could have sorted out the whole business.

11

How to Help Yourself

There are all kinds of reasons why people do not seek outside help for social anxiety. Partly it is a fear of others finding out if so far the shyness has been a secret. You may also fear ridicule, or being misunderstood even by your doctor who, you may feel, doesn't sympathize with your problem. Or you may fear nobody can do anything anyway. Or, if you want to help yourself over a difficulty rather than rely on others, you may not know what to do.

But you can help yourself. The first thing to do is to remind yourself that you are not the only person in the world to suffer from this problem. There are many others who, like you, hide their problem from the rest of the world and suffer for it. It is at least comforting to know that you are not unique. Next I suggest that you try to understand how your shyness came about and what form it takes. Imagine yourself trying to describe what is wrong with you to some sympathetic and interested listener who is asking you questions. You will find it much easier than to understand yourself, and you're half-way towards solving your problem.

The questions you have to ask are: What exactly is it that troubles you? Do you feel unhappy in all social situations or only some? If there are just some, then which ones? Are they eating with people, talking to people, meeting in groups, entering rooms with strangers, being watched at work and so on? If you feel uncomfortable in all social situations, what form does the discomfort take? Do you just feel uneasy and tongue-tied, wondering what to say to people, do you feel that people are looking at you all the time? Do you have distressing symptoms like nausea and shaking, sweating and so on? If you are in a group of people do you feel all right providing nobody pays you any attention and nothing is expected of you? Is it just when you feel that you should join in the conversation that you feel uncomfortable? Why? Is it because you do not know what to say or because you feel that nobody is going to be interested in your opinions anyway? Do you know what to say sometimes and not others? Are you all right in structured situations where you have a definite role and uncomfortable where it is free conversation, or is it the reverse? Do you feel that you are being put on the spot and scrutinized by people, and perhaps criticized unfairly? Do you feel that people frequently take the mickey out of you or do they ignore you?

By going through a series of questions like this you get nearer to understanding what actually is the matter with you. You may establish that you feel uncomfortable at mealtimes with other people, when you feel nauseous, tremble and become aware of other people round the table scrutinizing you. Having got that far you can go and ask more questions: Are there any things which help or make matters worse? Do you, for instance, feel better if you go with a particular friend or with your spouse? If the person you are going with knows about your problem do you feel better or worse? Do you ever feel trapped, particularly at a meeting or formal dinner? Do you feel uncomfortable at the cinema or theatre unless you are at the end of a row or right at the back? Can you manage to sit through the film without having to go out? If you have been to your doctor and talked about your problem, did he give you tablets and do they help? Are you all right at home, or when you are alone outside? Are you so self-conscious that you cannot go out unless it is dark or a grey day so that you will be less conspicuous? If you go to a gathering is it easier for you if it is informal, such as a buffet?

Next, you must look into the past and try to see how the problem came about. What sort of social life did your parents have? Did they entertain a lot or keep to themselves? If they had social gatherings did they include you? Were you made to feel comfortable or self-conscious? Were you excluded, so you had little chance to learn social skills? Did you have a disability such as a speech impediment or severe short-sightedness which distinguished you from the other children? All these things, and more, can add up to an unsatisfactory learning situation for the future, so that as an adult you are confronted with lack of experience or example from your parents to follow. Just knowing this can help you understand your problems now and may help you feel a little more tolerant towards yourself—shy people often blame themselves for their social difficulties when in fact it is wrapped up in the past, and if you can stop blaming yourself you will find it easier to analyse your problem and solve it.

Now try to work out what you want to achieve, being as careful as you can to avoid the stereotypes mentioned earlier. If you are not fundamentally the party-going type there is no reason why you should try to become one, it is just not appropriate for you. If you are a gentle, unaggressive male then don't try to become any different. If you feel uncomfortable about yourself physically try to get a simple book about the human body to see if you really are different from anyone else—you will probably find that you are not much different. Having eliminated the things you don't really want after all, you can decide what you really want to do. Perhaps it is as simple as being able to visit friends in comfort, have meals with them and invite them round to your house, or to go to club meetings and the local pub. Sort out all these items and turn them into a list, which might look something like the following:

1   Pay the milkman without trembling.
2   Visit next door neighbour for a cup of coffee.
3   Go into a shop and ask for a specific item which may need careful discussion and trouble for the shop assistant.
4   Go to a local pub with a friend.
5   Go to a disco.
6   Write a cheque in the bank without trembling hands.
7   Join in a coffee break at work.
8   Be able to do simple jobs with someone looking on.
9   Go to an informal restaurant with husband or wife.
10   Go to a similar restaurant with friends.
11   Attend parent–teachers' association meetings.
12   Attend other functions, such as plays, at children's schools.
13   Have a weekend in a hotel.
14   Go on holiday with friends.
15   Go to a large, formal dinner party.

This is simply an example. Your own list may be much different, but it should give you some idea. You will notice that the items are to some extent in order of difficulty; for most people a large formal dinner party is far more difficult than visiting friends for coffee.

Now that you have your list, you have to use it. You should think of your self-help programme as a type of correspondence course in which you might be learning maths or another language. I want to emphasize the *learning* because it can mean either learning for the first time or re-educating yourself to cope with situations which have become troublesome. There are probably many things that you prefer to avoid and if so, it is extremely hard for you to appreciate how you can learn to cope with them. This is one reason why you have to proceed in steps, as you would if you were learning a language. You start with very simple situations—those that you are on the edge of being able to do or can do with a little difficulty—and then move on to the more difficult ones. You are gradually climbing a ladder where you do not go on to the next rung until you are firmly settled on the first and quite sure that it is firm. Tackling difficult situations immediately will only discourage you.

Before you start, plan your campaign very carefully and try to see all the snags that may arise before you arrive, then you will be armed to deal with them. And don't wait too long before putting your plan into action. Try not to make your date too far ahead so that you get steamed up about it beforehand and cancel it.

Now that you have worked out your plan, you need to think ahead of various things that you might say which might interest somebody else and to think up questions that you might ask. People are always happy to talk about themselves, but usually they need an opening. You should also limit the time of your encounter so that it does not extend indefinitely into the future, making you feel unhappy and uncomfortable. Think of a plausible excuse so that you can leave at any time you feel that you want to. You might say that you have to get dinner ready, get something from the shop, do a load of washing or anything else that seems reasonable. Excuses are very important and are not the same as lies. They let you limit a potentially exhausting situation and they may be as much relief to the other person as they are to you (though you must make your excuse plausible so that it doesn't insult the other person's intelligence).

Say that you have decided to visit the pub; what do you do when you get there? There will probably be scattered groups of people there, some of them certainly on their own. Perhaps you find yourself comfortably next to somebody else on their own, or you may be next to a couple of people who know each other but are not intensely involved in a discussion. Then you can stand by, look interested, perhaps nod at some point that appeals to you and, eventually, be drawn into the conversation. It is often enough just to look interested, though if you look too intense and anxious, and if your expression is tense and your voice strained, your anxiety will be detected. If you make a deliberate effort to appear nonchalant, this will register and make it easier for others to draw you in. Remember, people feel threatened by anxiety because they often do not understand it.

If there is an obvious lull in the conversation or you are next to another loner, ask a general question such as whether there is a darts club, or do pop groups ever play here, conveying that you are interested in the pub rather than curious about the other person. You can then make a positive revelation such as 'I've just moved to this district.' This is a signal for a revelation from the other person. If he doesn't respond you could ask, 'Have you lived here long?' and if he says he has you can still keep the topic general by asking if it has changed much. If the answer is 'Yes' you can ask him how he finds it and whether he is happy with the move. All the time you are giving him the chance to tell you something about himself, but leaving him the option to avoid it if he wishes, so that if he is shy too he will not feel threatened. Your revelations must be suitably neutral at first. It would not

85

be a good plan at this stage to say that your wife has just left you or that your father has died. Until the other person knows you better he will not quite know how to cope with this sort of very intimate information.

Perhaps by now you have managed to get round to where you work and what you feel about your job, how you spend your spare time. If so, you will be doing very well. Now is probably the time to take your leave, as it is always best to do this when the atmosphere is still good rather than when ominous silences have started to appear. If you have still not exchanged names you could say, 'Oh, by the way, what's your name? Mine is Bill Taylor.' He might reply with his name, then you say, 'Right, Jack, I must be getting home, maybe I'll see you again.' Now that you have made your exit, having made a good encounter which can be followed up later, the next time you meet you will certainly be able to disclose more intimate information to each other.

If you find in these encounters that you do not actually take to the person very much then by having kept the conversation general you will not have committed yourself in any way. It is best not to appear too friendly until you are sure of yourself, because it is much more difficult to back out if you have made definite advances. Next time you go to the pub, for example, you can try talking to someone else, giving your previous acquaintances a friendly nod—or bringing them into the conversation with a new friend.

You can see that making friends with people is rather like tackling your problem in general: go one step at a time rather cautiously, feeling your way. The socially anxious person is so worried in case people will not like him that he does not reflect for a moment that he might not like the person he is trying to be friendly with, so leave yourself room for manoeuvre so as to avoid hurting feelings. Fortunately if people are going to get on the feeling is usually mutual, so if they aren't suited no further moves are made by either.

Having successfully made your first acquaintance at the pub, or when you are picking up your children from school, what do you do next? There are all sorts of things apart from having people round for meals at your home, which might be difficult at this early stage. You could arrange to go out to an informal restaurant with your respective partners, arrange to take the children for a drive, go to the zoo or the cinema, or anything else that you might fancy.

If, after assessing your problem, you have decided that you lack social skills—that you do not know how to behave with other people—you can go further than self-help and go to an out-patient clinic at a hospital to be taught. In the next chapter I will describe how this is done, and the advice there can also be used if you have definitely decided to try self-help.

There are other ways in which you can help yourself. All kinds of groups and associations exist which you can join if you can pluck up enough courage. This is where anti-anxiety pills from your doctor would make a great deal of difference, providing you take them three-quarters of an hour before you go on your particular adventure, rather than taking them as a regular rule. Most socially anxious people are only anxious in anticipation of the problems they face. If you have planned a campaign as I have suggested and you take a pill then your anxiety will be much less in the preceding hours and days before the event—simply knowing you have the pill to take if you need it can sometimes add confidence.

For people with specific problems there are clubs; the

Cruse Clubs for widows and widowers, Singles Clubs, church groups, and groups with special interests such as Ramblers' Associations, who explore the countryside on foot. There are also music clubs, discos, record clubs and perhaps you have a local theatre club. Once you have decided what you are interested in, and what sort of things you would enjoy doing with others, you can go to the Citizens' Advice Bureau and ask them for a list of associations or clubs in your area; they are always very helpful and have lots of information at their fingertips. These associations are very good because you do not have to converse with people all the time. You are doing something with people rather than being thrown in without any structure at all, and this makes it much easier to get to know people. If you feel you are ignorant about the particular topic you have decided on then you can always go to your local library and find some books about it. Never mind admitting that you are ignorant of something, regard your meetings as an opportunity to learn from others and perhaps to teach them something yourself.

Then there are groups with even more involvement in a particular activity, such as evening classes for English, pottery, metalwork or whatever. Decide if there is something which you would like to learn more about and which will be useful to you. You may find that you will go for weeks without talking to anybody, but you have to make the effort and you are at least among people with a very definite aim, and you are doing something fairly specific with them; this gives you the opportunity to strike up a conversation at any time you like.

A number of fringe movements, too, can be helpful if used with discrimination. One of these is transcendental meditation, very often confused with other forms of meditation and often misunderstood. It is not a religion, it is a technique for helping people to relax and overcome anxiety. If you are the sort of person who finds difficulty seeking help from anyone else or keeping to a regular schedule, then transcendental meditation might be very useful. All you have to do is to learn the technique from a local centre and go away and practise it for twenty minutes twice a day, not a lot of time to spend. Many people who have done this have been relieved of great anxiety and find they get on better with others as a result.

Now, having described how you can help yourself, we will move on to how you can get help from others. In the long run, even using advice is helping yourself, but others can speed your progress.

12

How to Get Help from Others

Many people who have social anxiety do not seek help, or try in a half-hearted way and are disappointed. There are good reasons for this and it is worth looking at all of them to clear the ground before we look at what help is available, how to get it and what it will be like.

Shyness or anxiety in social situations is often rather vague. You may have recurrent symptoms such as nausea, diarrhoea, tension or low spirits without connecting these feelings with social situations. We have already seen what a variety of responses people can can have and it is easy to think that you are suffering from a 'tummy bug' or that for some reason you are not quite on top form. Recurrent symptoms affecting your appetite or bowels for which there is no physical cause must be due to anxiety of some kind, but to sort this out with a busy doctor is rather daunting. This is one reason why people do not ask for help—they are not quite sure what the trouble is and find it hard to express.

Other people may know that every time they are asked out or someone comes round for a cup of coffee their heart pounds, they sweat and want to run away as fast as they can. However, they feel that this is foolish: for a man doing a responsible job it is shaming to have to admit that he needs several stiff drinks before he can go to a board meeting or interview and entertain a rep. These people believe that they are not really ill, that there are other people who need help more, that it is not the sort of problem to bother the doctor with and that they ought to be able to get over it themselves anyway. Of course they are right in not regarding this as an illness. It is an emotional disturbance which is exaggerated or inappropriate. We can liken it to the crippling fear which assails some susceptible person when they see a large spider. It is not an illness, but it is inconvenient and difficult to get over by yourself. Similarly, avoiding social situations because you are anxious or afraid that you are bound to make a fool of yourself is more than inconvenient—it can ruin your life. Also it is very hard to get over by yourself without special instructions.

So where should you go? The doctor does not seem to be a logical choice and nor is a psychiatrist, since they are supposed to deal with physical illness (or, in the latter case, mental illness). In fact both doctors and psychiatrists have broadened their scope to such an extent over the last ten years or more, that they see people whose problems are primarily emotional almost as much as they see people who are physically ill. A general practitioner will see children with sore throats or people with diabetes or high blood pressure and so forth, but for any two of these he will see someone who cannot sleep, who has lost interest in life, is overwrought, has marital strife or who is getting over the death of a close relative. There are others who have symptoms of anxiety for no apparent reason, people who are depressed or have agoraphobia. Social anxiety is just another on the list. Nevertheless, not all doctors are sympathetic to emotional problems and it is still possible to meet with a 'snap out of it' or 'you'll grow out of it' response. Even if he does recognize that there is something distressing, it may be outside his knowledge so he has to ask you to return for him to find out more about the problem and what treatment is available. He may even feel upset that he does not know how to help you and express this as a rebuff—doctors are human too! This is when you need to know what the problem is and express yourself clearly, saying that you know there are ways of treating it.

Another reason why people do not ask for help is because they are fairly sure that there is nothing available. Until a few years ago this was true and, unfortunately, it is still true for some areas, though more psychiatrists and clinical psychologists are being trained in the most up-to-date methods. Your doctor may not know that a particular treatment is now available in your area, but there are ways of finding out and if your own doctor is too busy you can contact the Patients' Association, your local Community Health Centre or see a notice of services in your area.

But let us suppose that your doctor is sympathetic and reasonably understanding and that he gives you a helpful talk about your problem. He may very well say some of the things that I have mentioned in the last chapter. He will probably give you tranquillizers and these are all very much the same, except that Valium, one of the most common, may make you drowsy, in which case you should ask for something else. There are plenty of tranquillizers that do not make people feel drowsy. Some are short-acting (four to six hours) others are long-acting (twenty-four hours). Make sure you find out from your doctor what specific properties belong to the tranquillizer he has prescribed for you. The long-acting tranquillizers are best taken at night if you have some anxiety provoking situation to face in the morning, or if you tend to feel anxious most of the time. On the whole they are not so good because you are not able to monitor your progress. With any kind of pill you should aim to take them in the earlier stages of your experiments until you are sufficiently confident to drop them, resuming them when you reach the next, more difficult stage. With long-acting tranquillizers you cannot do this, so you don't have the confidence-boosting advantage of knowing how you are progressing.

Your doctor may send you away with a bit of a chat, encouragement and pills, or he may decide to send you to the local hospital. Do not be daunted by this: remember that you are a consumer and that you have a right to say 'No' if you do not want to take advantage of what the hospital has to offer. You may like to go once for a long discussion, however, since hospitals generally try to give you an hour to assess your problem properly, which is far more than a general practitioner can afford. After this you may prefer to take matters into your own hands and try on your own—a semi self-help programme where you can report back every month just to say how you are getting on. Many psychiatrists like working in this way. At these sorts of interview you sort out goals in the way I described in the last chapter, making a careful list of them and deciding which are the easiest to tackle first. When you have had a shot at them, you report back and either go on to the next one or try a bit harder with slightly different tactics. Your confidence will probably increase by leaps and bounds and you will wonder what you were worrying about.

You may be invited to join a group, in which case you must find out very carefully what sort of group it is. Is it a group of other people with social anxiety or is it a large mixed group of people with all kinds of different complaints? If it is the latter then you would do well to refuse unless there is nothing else available. If, on the other hand, it is a group of people with social anxiety who are getting together with the express aim of practising situations which they all find difficult, you will find this immensely helpful.

The usual form these groups take is of between six and eight people who are chosen specifically and who have the same kind of problem. Each person will be seen individually in the first instance so that his problem can be carefully examined. At the first group meeting it is agreed that everybody has uncomfortable symptoms which will not be discussed, because this is not particularly helpful, but that all have definite goals they want to achieve and that a programme will be worked out by the group so that everybody's goals can be achieved in the long run.

There will usually be between eight and ten group meetings of this kind, with follow-ups afterwards, either individually or as a group. The practice depends very much on the group leader. Sometimes he or she will arrange for you to act out certain situations between yourselves. Let us say that five members of a group constitute a meeting and the sixth has to come and join in, making it as realistic as possible. Or you may all be given cups of coffee or one person may be detailed to make the coffee for the rest. Then you may act out going into shops, having meals in people's homes, restaurants and so on. There is almost no situation which cannot be acted out in some way and this is much the easiest way of dealing with it. Other group leaders set people real-life tasks like going into pubs and so on. This is more difficult because there are a limited number of situations which can be acted out in this way, but whichever way the group leader chooses there will be plenty of time for rehearsal and discussion beforehand so that you have a plan of attack before you set off. Generally the group leader is a clinical psychologist, but it could also be a social worker, a nurse or a psychiatrist. After something like eight sessions you will then be encouraged to try more tasks on your own and you will have already been told to practise as much as you can yourself.

An entirely different type of treatment is what is called *desensitization*. This is used mostly for people who have very definite symptoms, such as palpitations, sweating, diarrhoea, nausea and so on. It is unlikely to be given to people with mild social unease who simply have trouble knowing what to say to people. These people with definite physical symptoms are called social phobics. First of all, as in every form of treatment, you are asked to list the situations you find difficult and put them in order of anxiety. You will probably have something like ten to fifteen items. Then you are asked to lie on a couch or sit in a very comfortable chair and encouraged to relax. This is done by a sort of hypnotic technique although you are fully awake, alert and in control of the situation the whole time. You are never actually put into a state of trance, so if you are the sort of person who fears losing your control you have nothing to worry about.

The therapist will talk to you in a soothing voice, encouraging you to relax your muscles and helping you to feel warm, secure and peaceful. When you are quite relaxed—this in itself may take two or three sessions, though it is often successful the first time—you will be asked to imagine the easiest item in your hierarchy, say, opening the door to a tradesman. You will be asked to imagine this while you are relaxed and as soon as you become tense you will be asked to stop imagining it and to return to your state of relaxation, so that you are never allowed to become anxious while you are imagining these situations. When you have managed to imagine your task without being anxious on two or three occasions, you are

95

then encouraged to try the next item on your hierarchy. This kind of treatment is called *imaginal* desensitization, and at the same time you will probably be given instructions as to how to cope with anxiety when you are out and about.

Let us suppose that you are facing the situation of asking for time off. Go as soon as you possibly can, so that there is no time for your anxiety to build up. Concentrate on breathing regularly but not too deeply. When you get to the foreman's office concentrate on him and various things in his office rather than on how you feel. You will find in general that concentrating on what is *outside* yourself makes you far less anxious than allowing yourself to be sidetracked by your own fears and symptoms which will escalate as you concentrate on them. While you are having imaginal desensitization, probably six to eight sessions, you will be encouraged to try something out every day that you find difficult, gradually working your way up to those tasks which at the moment you find almost impossible.

Imaginal exposure is sometimes called implosion or flooding, but do not be put off by its unpleasant title. In the early days of this treatment, people were made to imagine the most anxiety-provoking situations that they could and went through a great deal of discomfort as a result. Now it is realized that it is sufficient to imagine less anxiety-provoking situations and therefore to experience less anxiety throughout the treatment. Nevertheless you may find one or two people who are still practising in the old way and who will encourage you to feel as anxious as possible. This treatment is effective because it makes you rehearse those situations which you have been frightened of tackling or whose implications you have not yet been able to examine. What you are asked to do then is to imagine joining the others at work for a coffee break; you will be asked to describe the room, the people, what they do, what they look like, the sort of things they might say, how you feel yourself in the situation, what you are frightened of and what you feel you may do which will attract adverse comment. During this rehearsal you may become quite anxious, but at the same time you will realize that your fears are nothing like as well grounded as you thought they were. There is nothing like looking at a situation in minute detail to dispel nameless fear. You will then have a discussion with the therapist on how to cope with the situation in real life and you will then be encouraged to go away and have a go at it.

Social skills training is another form of treatment and it will depend on precisely what your problems are. Let us say you are very poor on social skills and that you have no idea how to listen to people or how to express what you want to say. You will be given lessons, either by yourself or with a group of other people with similar problems, as to how to listen to people, how to look at them in the right way, how to alter your expression to be encouraging or discouraging as you wish, how to put people at ease and generally how to be a good listener. Then you will be instructed how to express what you wish to say to another person, encouraged to talk about yourself, giving graded information starting with the general and gradually leading to the more intimate. Then specific problems, like first encounters, ending encounters, making arrangements for further meetings and so on, will be dealt with. Following this you will be encouraged to act out certain situations such as going for an interview for a job. If you are very poor on social skills this can all take rather a long time and you should not be discouraged if treatment takes more than a year. You must remember that this has been a lifelong problem, and it is not going to be solved in a week. You may feel you are making no progress, but if you persevere you will eventually arrive at a gratifying breakthrough where you find you are doing very much better than you ever thought possible.

These are the main forms of treatment and you should not hesitate to ask the psychiatrist or clinical psychologist to describe in more detail precisely what methods are used in that particular clinic. You may be offered drugs at the same time to be used in the way that I have described and though these can be very helpful, do not hesitate to refuse them if you are definitely anti-drug.

Various self-help groups have been formed to help people overcome particular problems, and these can make it quite clear in the early stages that other people have the same difficulties as you have. Most have a regular news-letter in which members express their difficulties. The main ones that spring to mind are The Phobic Society, The Open Door and Neurotics Anonymous. The Open Door is mainly for agoraphobics, but they do have social phobic members as well. Neurotics Anonymous, although it is for any kind of phobic, tends to be predominantly agoraphobic, partly because agoraphobia was recognized some time ago as a particular problem. Though they are easily confused (it's easy to see why, since both groups fear going into shops, walking in the street and so forth) their fears are not identical: agoraphobics are frightened of some personal catastrophe and are relieved if there are other people around; social phobics, on the other hand, are worried about scrutiny and so are relieved if they are alone.

Now that we have come to an end of our detailed excursion into social anxiety, all that remains is to summarize what we have covered.

Postscript

People of all kinds can suffer from social anxiety and anyone writing for them has to aim for the middle course. I have tried to give a picture of the setting of social anxiety, how it emerges, types of social anxiety and what to do about it.

By and large, in our society where there are few rules and little is taught in the formal way, we have to learn by trial and error. This means it takes quite a lot of courage and it is not easy for any of us to learn social confidence easily. Knowing this will perhaps help you be more tolerant of your own shortcomings.

But when all is said and done about social skills and how to improve them, and how to get over anxiety, what are we really trying to achieve? Ultimately we want satisfying relationships and these can only be had on a basis of complete honesty, with the reservation that you should make some effort to be considerate and help others save face. Honesty means trying to be as natural as we possibly can and as near to our real selves as we feel able.

This is a big problem and like other problems can seem daunting. If you read a book about marriage and parenthood before you marry and have children, you may feel it is simply not worth taking the risk, that the pitfalls are too great. But you must remember that people have been marrying, starting families and managing their social skills well enough for hundreds of years without reading books about it. We all have the resources to cope if we just use them. But books do give you an extra bit of help, so don't be put off using them to help you sort out your problem. Even if you have to read various parts of this book several times before you understand it perfectly, it's no reflection on your intelligence. So far little has been written about social anxiety, so you will be one of the first to try and tackle it in a systematic way.

Nor has there been much research on social phobia, though a recent study in Oxford shows that with help a number of people appear to have been completely cured and many others so much improved that their lives have changed out of all recognition. Few people were unchanged and nobody was made worse. Of those people who did not seem to make much progress on one kind of treatment, which gave them a mere ten visits, most improved greatly with more or different treatment. The few people who did not improve at all had other very major problems such as alcoholism or severe depression to cope with as well.

So you should start your own explorations and experiments, either on your own or with professional help with the knowledge that most people can overcome social anxiety, or at least ease it considerably. Think of it as an adventure. It is certainly a challenge. Good luck!

Further Reading

Argyle, Michael, *Bodily Communication*. Methuen 1975. International Universities Press, USA, 1975.

Argyle, Michael, *Social Encounters*. Penguin 1973. Aldine, USA, 1973.

Bowlby, John, *Child Care and the Growth of Love*. Penguin 1970.

Darwin, Charles, *The Expression of the Emotions in Man and Animals*. University of Chicago Press, 1965.

Erikson, Erik, *Identity: Youth and Crisis*. Faber 1971. Norton, USA, 1968.

Hall, Edward, *The Silent Language*. Doubleday 1973.

Hinde, Robert A., *Nonverbal Communication*. Cambridge University Press 1975.

Lorenz, Konrad, *Evolution and Modification of Behaviour*. Chicago University Press 1965.

Index